# TALES OF ATLANTIS

"Sometimes a maiden held up an apple of gold to Niam and Usheen as their slender white horse dashed across the waves of the ocean." —p. 27

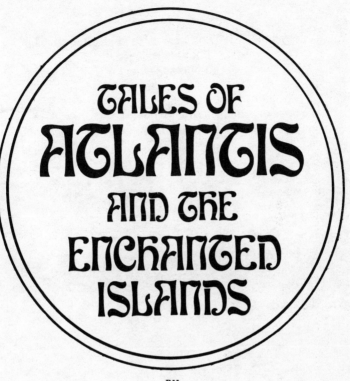

# TALES OF ATLANTIS AND THE ENCHANTED ISLANDS

BY

THOMAS WENTWORTH HIGGINSON

With Illustrations by Albert Herter

" Mediæval maps swarmed with fabulous islands; and wild stories of adventurous voyages divided the attention with tales of love and war." — *Winsor's " Narrative and Critical History of America," I, 31.*

NEWCASTLE PUBLISHING COMPANY, INC.
NORTH HOLLYWOOD, CALIFORNIA

1977

Original title:
*Tales of the Enchanted Islands of the Atlantic*

A NEWCASTLE BOOK
FIRST PRINTING OCTOBER 1977
PRINTED IN THE UNITED STATES OF AMERICA

TO

**General Sir George Wentworth Higginson, K.C.B.**

*Gyldernscroft, Marlow, England*

---

THIS BOOK IS INSCRIBED, IN TOKEN OF KINDRED AND OF
OLD FAMILY FRIENDSHIPS, CORDIALLY PRESERVED
INTO THE PRESENT GENERATION

---

THESE LEGENDS UNITE THE TWO SIDES OF THE ATLANTIC
AND FORM A PART OF THE COMMON HERITAGE
OF THE ENGLISH-SPEAKING RACE

# Preface

HAWTHORNE in his *Wonder Book* has described the beautiful Greek myths and traditions, but no one has yet made similar use of the wondrous tales that gathered for more than a thousand years about the islands of the Atlantic deep. Although they are a part of the mythical period of American history, these hazy legends were altogether disdained by the earlier historians; indeed, George Bancroft made it a matter of actual pride that the beginning of the American annals was bare and literal. But in truth no national history has been less prosaic as to its earlier traditions, because every visitor had to cross the sea to reach it, and the sea has always been, by the mystery of its horizon, the fury of its storms, and the variableness of the atmosphere above it, the foreordained land of romance.

In all ages and with all sea-going races there has always been something especially fascinating about an island amid the ocean. Its very existence has for all explorers an air of magic. An island offers to us heights rising from depths; it

exhibits that which is most fixed beside that
which is most changeable, the fertile beside the
barren, and safety after danger. The ocean forever tends to encroach on the island, the island
upon the ocean. They exist side by side, friends
yet enemies. The island signifies safety in calm,
and yet danger in storm; in a tempest the sailor
rejoices that he is not near it; even if previously
bound for it, he puts about and steers for the open
sea. Often if he seeks it he cannot reach it. The
present writer spent a winter on the island of
Fayal, and saw in a storm a full-rigged ship drift
through the harbor disabled, having lost her an-
chors; and it was a week before she again made
the port.

There are groups of islands scattered over the
tropical ocean, especially, to which might well be
given Herman Melville's name, "Las Encantadas," the Enchanted Islands. These islands,
usually volcanic, have no vegetation but cactuses
or wiry bushes with strange names; no inhabitants
but insects and reptiles — lizards, spiders, snakes,
— with vast tortoises which seem of immemorial
age, and are coated with seaweed and the slime of
the ocean. If there are any birds, it is the strange
and heavy penguin, the passing albatross, or the
Mother Cary's chicken, which has been called the
humming bird of ocean, and here finds a place for

its young. By night these birds come for their
repose; at earliest dawn they take wing and
hover over the sea, leaving the isle deserted.
The only busy or beautiful life which always sur-
rounds it is that of a myriad species of fish, of all
forms and shapes, and often more gorgeous than
any butterflies in gold and scarlet and yellow.

Once set foot on such an island and you begin
at once to understand the legends of enchantment
which ages have collected around such spots.
Climb to its heights, you seem at the masthead
of some lonely vessel, kept forever at sea. You
feel as if no one but yourself had ever landed
there; and yet, perhaps, even there, looking
straight downward, you see below you in some
crevice of the rock a mast or spar of some
wrecked vessel, encrusted with all manner of
shells and uncouth vegetable growth. No matter how distant the island or how peacefully it
seems to lie upon the water, there may be perplexing currents that ever foam and swirl about
it — currents which are, at all tides and in the
calmest weather, as dangerous as any tempest, and
which make compass untrustworthy and helm
powerless. It is to be remembered also that an
island not only appears and disappears upon the
horizon in brighter or darker skies, but it varies
its height and shape, doubles itself in mirage, or

looks as if broken asunder, divided into two or three. Indeed the buccaneer, Cowley, writing of one such island which he had visited, says: "My fancy led me to call it Cowley's Enchanted Isle, for we having had a sight of it upon several points of the compass, it appeared always in so many different forms; sometimes like a ruined fortification; upon another point like a great city."

If much of this is true even now, it was far truer before the days of Columbus, when men were constantly looking westward across the Atlantic, and wondering what was beyond. In those days, when no one knew with certainty whether the ocean they observed was a sea or a vast lake, it was often called "The Sea of Darkness." A friend of the Latin poet, Ovid, describing the first approach to this sea, says that as you sail out upon it the day itself vanishes, and the world soon ends in perpetual darkness:—

> "Quo ferimur? Ruit ipsa dies, orbemque relictum
> Ultima perpetuis claudit natura tenebris."

Nevertheless, it was the vague belief of many nations that the abodes of the blest lay somewhere beyond it — in the "other world," a region half earthly, half heavenly, whence the spirits of the departed could not cross the water to return; — and so they were constantly imagining excursions made by favored mortals to enchanted islands. To add to the confusion, actual islands in the Atlantic were sometimes discovered and actually lost again, as, for instance, the Canaries, which were reached and called the Fortunate Isles a little before the Christian era, and were then lost to sight for thirteen centuries ere being visited again.

The glamour of enchantment was naturally first attached by Europeans to islands within sight of their own shores — Irish, Welsh, Breton, or Spanish, — and then, as these islands became better known, men's imaginations carried the mystery further out over the unknown western sea. The line of legend gradually extended itself till it formed an imaginary chart for Columbus; the aged astronomer, Toscanelli, for instance, suggesting to him the advantage of making the supposed island of Antillia a half-way station; just as it was proposed, long centuries after, to find a station for the ocean telegraph in the equally imaginary island of Jacquet, which has only lately disappeared from the charts. With every step in knowledge the line of fancied stopping-places rearranged itself, the fictitious names flitting from place to place on the maps, and sometimes duplicating themselves. Where the tradition itself has

vanished we find that the names with which it
associated itself are still assigned, as in case of
Brazil and the Antilles, to wholly different
localities.

The order of the tales in the present work follows roughly the order of development, giving
first the legends which kept near the European
shore, and then those which, like St. Brandan's
or Antillia, were assigned to the open sea or, like
Norumbega or the Isle of Demons, to the very
coast of America. Every tale in this book bears
reference to some actual legend, followed more or
less closely, and the authorities for each will be
found carefully given in the appendix for such
readers as may care to follow the subject farther.
It must be remembered that some of these imaginary islands actually remained on the charts of
the British admiralty until within a century. If
even the exact science of geographers retained
them thus long, surely romance should embalm
them forever.

# Contents

# List of Illustrations

xv

# I

## THE STORY OF ATLANTIS

THE Greek sage Socrates, when he was but a boy minding his father's goats, used to lie on the grass under the myrtle trees; and, while the goats grazed around him, he loved to read over and over the story which Solon, the law-giver and poet, wrote down for the great-grandfather of Socrates, and which Solon had always meant to make into a poem, though he died without doing it. But this was briefly what he wrote in prose: —

"I, Solon, was never in my life so surprised as when I went to Egypt for instruction in my youth, and there, in the temple of Sais, saw an aged priest who told me of the island of Atlantis, which was sunk in the sea thousands of years ago. He said that in the division of the earth the gods agreed that the god Poseidon, or Neptune, should have, as his share, this

great island which then lay in the ocean west
of the Mediterranean Sea, and was larger than
all Asia.    There was a mortal maiden there
whom Poseidon wished to marry, and to secure her he surrounded the valley where she
dwelt with three rings of sea and two of land
so that no one could enter; and he made
underground springs, with water hot or cold,
and supplied all things needful to the life of
man.    Here he lived with her for many years,
and they had ten sons; and these sons divided
the island among them and had many children,
who dwelt there for more than a thousand
years.    They had mines of gold and silver,
and pastures for elephants, and many fragrant
plants.    They erected palaces and dug canals;
and they built their temples of white, red, and
black stone, and covered them with gold and
silver.    In these were statues of gold, especially
one of the god Poseidon driving six winged
horses.    He was so large as to touch the roof
with his head, and had a hundred water-nymphs
around him, riding on dolphins.    The islanders
had also baths and gardens and sea-walls, and

they had twelve hundred ships and ten thousand
chariots. All this was in the royal city alone,
and the people were friendly and good and
well-affectioned towards all. But as time went
on they grew less so, and they did not obey
the laws, so that they offended heaven. In a
single day and night the island disappeared
and sank beneath the sea; and this is why
the sea in that region grew so impassable and
impenetrable, because there is a quantity of
shallow mud in the way, and this was caused
by the sinking of a single vast island.

"This is the tale," said Solon, "which the
old Egyptian priest told to me." And Solon's
tale was read by Socrates, the boy, as he lay
in the grass; and he told it to his friends after
he grew up, as is written in his dialogues recorded by his disciple, Plato. And though this
great island of Atlantis has never been seen
again, yet a great many smaller islands have
been found in the Atlantic Ocean, and they have
sometimes been lost to sight and found again.

There is, also, in this ocean a vast tract of
floating seaweed, called by sailors the Sargasso

Sea, — covering a region as large as France, — and this has been thought by many to mark the place of a sunken island. There are also many islands, such as the Azores, which have been supposed at different times to be fragments of Atlantis; and besides all this, the remains of the vanished island have been looked for in all parts of the world. Some writers have thought it was in Sweden, others in Spitzbergen, others in Africa, in Palestine, in America. Since the depth of the Atlantic has been more thoroughly sounded, a few writers have maintained that the inequalities of its floor show some traces of the submerged Atlantis, but the general opinion of men of science is quite the other way. The visible Atlantic islands are all, or almost all, they say, of volcanic origin; and though there are ridges in the bottom of the ocean, they do not connect the continents.

At any rate, this was the original story of Atlantis, and the legends which follow in these pages have doubtless all grown, more or less, out of this first tale which Socrates told.

## II

## TALIESSIN OF THE RADIANT BROW

IN times past there were enchanted islands in the Atlantic Ocean, off the coast of Wales, and even now the fishermen sometimes think they see them. On one of these there lived a man named Tegid Voel and his wife called Cardiwen. They had a son, the ugliest boy in the world, and Cardiwen formed a plan to make him more attractive by teaching him all possible wisdom. She was a great magician and resolved to boil a large caldron full of knowledge for her son, so that he might know all things and be able to predict all that was to happen. Then she thought people would value him in spite of his ugliness. But she knew that the caldron must burn a year and a day without ceasing, until three blessed drops of the water of knowledge were obtained from it; and those

5

three drops would give all the wisdom she wanted.

So she put a boy named Gwion to stir the caldron and a blind man named Morda to feed the fire; and made them promise never to let it cease boiling for a year and a day. She herself kept gathering magic herbs and putting them into it. One day when the year was nearly over, it chanced that three drops of the liquor flew out of the caldron and fell on the finger of Gwion. They were fiery hot, and he put his finger to his mouth, and the instant he tasted them he knew that they were the enchanted drops for which so much trouble had been taken. By their magic he at once foresaw all that was to come, and especially that Cardiwen the enchantress would never forgive him.

Then Gwion fled. The caldron burst in two, and all the liquor flowed forth, poisoning some horses which drank it. These horses belonged to a king named Gwyddno. Cardiwen came in and saw all the toil of the whole year lost. Seizing a stick of wood, she struck the blind man Morda fiercely on the head, but he said, " I am innocent. It was not I who did it." "True," said Cardiwen; "it was the boy Gwion who robbed me;" and she rushed to pursue him. He saw her and fled, changing into a hare; but she became a greyhound and followed him. Running to the water, he became a fish; but she became another and chased him below the waves. He turned himself into a bird, when she became a hawk and gave him no rest in the sky. Just as she swooped on him, he espied a pile of winnowed wheat on the floor of a barn, and dropping upon it, he became one of the wheat-grains. Changing herself into a high-crested black hen, Cardiwen scratched him up and swallowed him, when he changed at last into a boy again and was so beautiful that she could not kill him outright, but wrapped him in a leathern bag and cast him into the sea, committing him to the mercy of God. This was on the twenty-ninth of April.

Now Gwyddno had a weir for catching fish on the sea-strand near his castle, and every day in May he was wont to take a hundred pounds' worth of fish. He had a son named Elphin, who was always poor and unsuccessful, but that

year the father had given the son leave to draw
all the fish from the weir, to see if good luck
would ever befall him and give him something
with which to begin the world.

When Elphin went next to draw the weir, the
man who had charge of it said in pity, "Thou
art always unlucky; there is nothing in the weir
but a leathern bag, which is caught on one of
the poles." "How do we know," said Elphin,
"that it may not contain the value of a hundred
pounds?" Taking up the bag and opening it,
the man saw the forehead of the boy and said to
Elphin, "Behold, what a radiant brow" (Taliessin). "Let him be called Taliessin," said
Elphin. Then he lifted the boy and placed him
sorrowfully behind him; and made his horse
amble gently, that before had been trotting, and
carried him as softly as if he had been sitting in
the easiest chair in the world, and the boy of the
radiant brow made a song to Elphin as they went
along.

> "Never in Gwyddno's weir
> Was there such good luck as this night.
> Fair Elphin, dry thy cheeks!

Being too sad will not avail,
Although thou thinkest thou hast no gain.
Too much grief will bring thee no good;
Nor doubt the miracles of the Almighty:
Although I am but little, I am highly gifted.
From seas, and from mountains,
And from the depths of rivers,
God brings wealth to the fortunate man.
Elphin of lively qualities,
Thy resolution is unmanly:
Thou must not be oversorrowful:
Better to trust in God than to forebode ill.
Weak and small as I am,
On the foaming beach of the ocean,
In the day of trouble I shall be
Of more service to thee than three hundred salmon.
Elphin of notable qualities,
Be not displeased at thy misfortune:
Although reclined thus weak in my bag,
There lies a virtue in my tongue.
While I continue thy protector
Thou hast not much to fear."


Then Elphin asked him, " Art thou man or spirit?" And in answer the boy sang to him this tale of his flight from the woman: —

"I have fled with vigor, I have fled as a frog,
I have fled in the semblance of a crow scarcely finding
       rest;
I have fled vehemently, I have fled as a chain of light-
       ning,
I have fled as a roe into an entangled thicket;
I have fled as a wolf-cub, I have fled as a wolf in the
       wilderness,
I have fled as a fox used to many swift bounds and
       quirks;
I have fled as a martin, which did not avail;
I have fled as a squirrel that vainly hides,
I have fled as a stag's antler, of ruddy course,
I have fled as an iron in a glowing fire,
I have fled as a spear-head, of woe to such as have a
       wish for it;
I have fled as a fierce bull bitterly fighting,
I have fled as a bristly boar seen in a ravine,
I have fled as a white grain of pure wheat;
Into a dark leathern bag I was thrown,
And on a boundless sea I was sent adrift;
Which was to me an omen of being tenderly nursed,
And the Lord God then set me at liberty."


Then Elphin came with Taliessin to the house
of his father, and Gwyddno asked him if he had a
good haul at the fish-weir.    "I have something

better than fish." "What is that?" asked the
father. "I have a bard," said Elphin. "Alas,
what will he profit thee?" said Gwyddno, to
which Taliessin replied, "He will profit him
more than the weir ever profited thee." Said
Gwyddno, "Art thou able to speak, and thou
so little?" Then Taliessin said, "I am better
able to speak than thou to question me."

From this time Elphin always prospered, and
he and his wife cared for Taliessin tenderly and
lovingly, and the boy dwelt with him until he
was thirteen years old, when Elphin went to
make a Christmas visit to his uncle Maelgwyn,
who was a great king and held open court.
There were four and twenty bards there, and all
proclaimed that no king had a wife so beautiful
as the queen, or a bard so wise as the twenty-
four, who all agreed upon this decision. Elphin
said, on the contrary, that it was he himself who
had the most beautiful wife and the wisest bard,
and for this he was thrown into prison. Taliessin learning this, set forth from home to visit
the palace and free his adoptive father, Elphin.

In those days it was the custom of kings to

sit in the hall and dine in royal state with lords
and bards about them who should keep proclaiming the greatness and glory of the king and
his knights.  Taliessin placed himself in a quiet
corner, waiting for the four and twenty bards to
pass, and as each one passed by, Taliessin made
an ugly face, and gave a sound with his finger
on his lips, thus, "Blerwm, Blerwm."   Each bard
went by and bowed himself before the king, but
instead of beginning to chant his praises, could
only play " Blerwm, Blerwm " on the lips, as the
boy had done.  The king was amazed and
thought they must be intoxicated, so he sent one
of his lords to them, telling them to behave
themselves and remember where they were.
Twice and thrice he told them, but they could
only repeat the same foolishness, until at last the
king ordered one of his squires to give a blow to
the chief bard, and the squire struck him a blow
with a broom, so that he fell back on his seat.
Then he arose and knelt before the king, and
said, " Oh, honorable king, be it known unto
your grace that it is not from too much drinking
that we are dumb, but through the influence of a

spirit which sits in the corner yonder in the form
of a child." Then the king bade a squire to
bring Taliessin before him, and he asked the boy
who he was. He answered: —

" Primary chief bard I am to Elphin,
   And my original country is the region of the summer
       stars ;
   I am a wonder whose origin is not known;
   I have been fostered in the land of the Deity,
   I have been teacher to all intelligences,
   I am able to instruct the whole universe.
   I was originally little Gwion,
   And at length I am Taliessin."

Then the king and his nobles wondered much,
for they had never heard the like from a boy so
young. The king then called his wisest bard to
answer Taliessin, but he could only play
" Blerwm " on his lips as before, and each of the
king's four and twenty bards tried in the same
way and could do nothing more. Then the
king bade Taliessin sing again, and he began: —

     " Discover thou what is
      The strong creature from before the flood,

Without flesh, without bone,
Without vein, without blood,
Without head, without feet;
It will neither be older nor younger
Than at the beginning;
Great God! how the sea whitens
When first it comes!
Great are its gusts
When it comes from the south;
Great are its evaporations
When it strikes on coasts.
It is in the field, it is in the wood,
Without hand and without foot,
Without signs of old age,
It is also so wide,
As the surface of the earth;
And it was not born,
Nor was it seen.
It will cause consternation
Wherever God willeth.
On sea and on land
It neither sees, nor is seen.
Its course is devious,
And will not come when desired.
On land and on sea
It is indispensable.
It is without equal,

It is many-sided;
It is not confined,
It is incomparable;
It comes from four quarters;
It is noxious, it is beneficial;
It is yonder, it is here;
It will decompose,
But it will not repair the injury;
It will not suffer for its doings,
Seeing it is blameless.
One Being has prepared it,
Out of all creatures,
By a tremendous blast,
To wreak vengeance
On Maelgwyn Gwynedd."

And while he was thus singing his verse near the door, there came suddenly a mighty storm of wind, so that the king and all his nobles thought the castle would fall on their heads. They saw that Taliessin had not merely been singing the song of the wind, but seemed to have power to command it. Then the king hastily ordered that Elphin should be brought from his dungeon and placed before Taliessin, and the chains came loose from his feet, and he was set free.

As they rode away from the court, the king and his courtiers rode with them, and Taliessin bade Elphin propose a race with the king's horses. Four and twenty horses were chosen, and Taliessin got four and twenty twigs of holly which he had burnt black, and he ordered the youth who was to ride Elphin's horse to let all the others set off before him, and bade him as he overtook each horse to strike him with a holly twig and throw it down. Then he had him watch where his own horse should stumble and throw down his cap at the place. The race being won, Taliessin brought his master to the spot where the cap lay; and put workmen to dig a hole there. When they had dug deeply enough they found a caldron full of gold, and Taliessin said, " Elphin, this is my payment to thee for having taken me from the water and reared me until now." And on this spot stands a pool of water until this day.

# III

## THE SWAN-CHILDREN OF LIR

KING LIR of Erin had four young children who were cared for tenderly at first by their stepmother, the new queen; but there came a time when she grew jealous of the love their father bore them, and resolved that she would endure it no longer. Sometimes there was murder in her heart, but she could not bear the thought of that wickedness, and she resolved at last to choose another way to rid herself of them. One day she took them to drive in her chariot: — Finola, who was eight years old, with her three younger brothers, — Aodh, Fiacre, and little Conn, still a baby. They were beautiful children, the legend says, with skins white and soft as swans' feathers, and with large blue eyes and very sweet voices. Reaching a lake, she told them that they might bathe in the clear water; but so soon as they were in it she struck them with a fairy wand, — for she was of the race of the Druids, who had magical power, — and she turned them into four beautiful snow-white swans. But they still had human voices, and Finola said to her, "This wicked deed of thine shall be punished, for the doom that awaits thee will surely be worse than ours." Then Finola asked, "How long shall we be in the shape of swans?" "For three hundred years," said the woman, "on smooth Lake Darvra; then three hundred years on the sea of Moyle" (this being the sea between Ireland and Scotland); "and then three hundred years at Inis Glora, in the Great Western Sea" (this was a rocky island in the Atlantic). "Until the Tailkenn (St. Patrick) shall come to Ireland and bring the Christian faith, and until you hear the Christian bell, you shall not be freed. Neither your power nor mine can now bring you back to human shape; but you shall keep your human reason and your Gaelic speech, and you shall sing music so sweet that all who hear it shall gladly listen."

She left them, and ere long their father, King

Lir, came to the shore and heard their singing. He asked how they came to have human voices. "We are thy four children," said Finola, "changed into swans by our stepmother's jealousy." "Then come and live with me," said her sorrowing father. "We are not permitted to leave the lake," she said, "or live with our people any more. But we are allowed to dwell together and to keep our reason and our speech, and to sing sweet music to you." Then they sang, and the king and all his followers were at first amazed and then lulled to sleep.

Then King Lir returned and met the cruel stepmother at her father's palace. When her father, King Bove, was told what she had done, he was hot with anger. "This wicked deed," he said, "shall bring severer punishment on thee than on the innocent children, for their suffering shall end, but thine never shall." Then King Bove asked her what form of existence would be most terrible to her. She replied, "That of a demon of the air." "Be it so," said her father, who had also Druidical power. He struck her with his wand, and she became a bat, and flew away with a scream, and the legend says, " She is still a demon of the air and shall be a demon of the air until the end of time."

After this, the people of all the races that were in Erin used to come and encamp by the lake and listen to the swans. The happy were made happier by the song, and those who were in grief or illness or pain forgot their sorrows and were lulled to rest. There was peace in all that region, while war and tumult filled other lands. Vast changes took place in three centuries — towers and castles rose and fell, villages were built and destroyed, generations were born and died;—and still the swan-children lived and sang, until at the end of three hundred years they flew away, as was decreed, to the stormy sea of Moyle; and from that time it was made a law that no one should kill a swan in Erin.

Beside the sea of Moyle they found no longer the peaceful and wooded shores they had known, but only steep and rocky coasts and a wild, wild sea. There came a great storm one night, and the swans knew that they could not keep together, so they resolved that if separated they would meet at a rock called Carricknarone. Finola reached there first, and took her brothers under her wings, all wet, shivering, and exhausted. Many such nights followed, and in one terrible winter storm, when they nestled together on Carricknarone, the water froze into solid ice around them, and their feet and wings were so frozen to the rock that when they moved they left the skin of their feet, the quills of their wings, and the feathers of their breasts clinging there. When the ice melted, and they swam out into the sea, their bodies smarted with pain until the feathers grew once more.

One day they saw a glittering troop of horsemen approaching along the shore and knew that they were their own kindred, though from far generations back, the Dedannen or Fairy Host. They greeted each other with joy, for the Fairy Host had been sent to seek for the swans; and on returning to their chiefs they narrated what had passed, and the chiefs said, "We cannot help them, but we are glad they are living; and we know that at last the enchantment will be broken and that they will be freed from their sorrows." So passed their lives until Finola sang, one day, "The Second Woe has passed — the second period of three hundred years," when they flew out on the broad ocean, as was decreed, and went to the island of Inis Glora. There they spent the next three hundred years, amid yet wilder storms and yet colder winds. No more the peaceful shepherds and living neighbors were around them; but often the sailor and fisherman, in his little coracle, saw the white gleam of their wings or heard the sweet notes of their song and knew that the children of Lir were near.

But the time came when the nine hundred years of banishment were ended, and they might fly back to their father's old home, Finnahà. Flying for days above the sea, they alighted at the palace once so well known, but everything was changed by time — even the walls of their father's palace were crumbled and rain-washed. So sad was the sight that they remained one day only, and flew back to Inis Glora, thinking that if they must be forever solitary, they would live where they had lived last, not where they had been reared.

One May morning, as the children of Lir floated in the air around the island of Inis Glora, they heard a faint bell sounding across the eastern sea. The mist lifted, and they saw afar off, beyond the waves, a vision of a stately white-robed priest, with attendants around him on the Irish shore. They knew that it must be St. Patrick, the Tailkenn, or Tonsured One, who was bringing, as had been so long promised, Christianity to Ireland. Sailing through the air, above the blue sea, towards their native coast, they heard the bell once more, now near and distinct, and they knew that all evil spirits were fleeing away, and that their own hopes were to be fulfilled. As they approached the land, St. Patrick stretched his hand and said, "Children of Lir, you may tread your native land again." And the sweet swan-sister, Finola, said, "If we tread our native land, it can only be to die, after our life of nine centuries. Baptize us while we are yet living." When they touched the shore, the weight of all those centuries fell upon them; they resumed their human bodies, but they appeared old and pale and wrinkled. Then St. Patrick bap-

tized them, and they died; but, even as he did
so, a change swiftly came over them; and they
lay side by side, once more children, in their
white night-clothes, as when their father Lir,
long centuries ago, had kissed them at evening
and seen their blue eyes close in sleep and had
touched with gentle hand their white foreheads
and their golden hair.   Their time of sorrow was
ended and their last swan-song was sung; but
the cruel stepmother seems yet to survive in her
bat-like shape, and a single glance at her weird
and malicious little face will lead us to doubt
whether she has yet fully atoned for her sin.

## IV

## USHEEN IN THE ISLAND OF YOUTH

THE old Celtic hero and poet Usheen
or Oisin, whose supposed songs are
known in English as those of Ossian,
lived to a great old age, surviving all others of
the race of the Feni, to which he belonged; and
he was asked in his last years what had given him
such length of life. This is the tale he told: —

After the fatal battle of Gavra, in which most
of the Feni were killed, Usheen and his father,
the king, and some of the survivors of the battle
were hunting the deer with their dogs, when they
met a maiden riding on a slender white horse
with hoofs of gold, and with a golden crescent
between his ears. The maiden's hair was of the
color of citron and was gathered in a silver band;
and she was clad in a white garment embroidered
with strange devices. She asked them why they

rode slowly and seemed sad, and not like other hunters; and they replied that it was because of the death of their friends and the ruin of their race. When they asked her in turn whence she came, and why, and whether she was married, she replied that she had never had a lover or a husband, but that she had crossed the sea for the love of the great hero and bard Usheen, whom she had never seen. Then Usheen was overcome with love for her, but she said that to wed her he must follow her across the sea to the Island of Perpetual Youth. There he would have a hundred horses and a hundred sheep and a hundred silken robes, a hundred swords, a hundred bows, and a hundred youths to follow him; while she would have a hundred maidens to wait on her. But how, he asked, was he to reach this island? He was to mount her horse and ride behind her. So he did this, and the slender white horse, not feeling his weight, dashed across the waves of the ocean, which did not yield beneath his tread. They galloped across the very sea, and the maiden, whose name was Niam, sang to him as they rode, and this so enchantingly that he

scarcely knew whether hours passed or days.
Sometimes deer ran by them over the water, followed by red-eared hounds in full chase; sometimes a maiden holding up an apple of gold;
sometimes a beautiful youth; but they themselves rode on always westward.

At last they drew near an island which was
not, Niam said, the island they were seeking;
but it was one where a beautiful princess was
kept under a spell until some defender should
slay a cruel giant who held her under enchantment until she should either wed him or furnish
a defender.  The youth Usheen, being an Irish-
man and not easily frightened, naturally offered
his services as defender, and they waited three
days and nights to carry on the conflict.  He
had fought at home — so the legend says — with
wild boars, with foreign invaders, and with enchanters, but he never had quite so severe a
contest as with this giant; but after he had cut
off his opponent's head and had been healed with
precious balm by the beautiful princess, he buried
the giant's body in a deep grave and placed
above it a great stone engraved in the Ogham

alphabet — in which all the letters are given in straight lines.

After this he and Niam again mounted the white steed and galloped away over the waves. Niam was again singing, when soft music began to be heard in the distance, as if in the centre of the setting sun. They drew nearer and nearer to a shore where the very trees trembled with the multitude of birds that sang upon them; and when they reached the shore, Niam gave one note of song, and a band of youths and maidens came rushing towards them and embraced them with eagerness. Then they too sang, and as they did it, one brought to Usheen a harp of silver and bade him sing of earthly joys. He found himself chanting, as he thought, with peculiar spirit and melody, but as he told them of human joys they kept still and began to weep, till at last one of them seized the silver harp and flung it away into a pool of water, saying, "It is the saddest harp in all the world."

Then he forgot all the human joys which seemed to those happy people only as sorrows compared with their own; and he dwelt with

them thenceforward in perpetual youth.  For a
hundred years he chased the deer and went fishing in strangely carved boats and joined in the
athletic sports of the young men; for a hundred
years the gentle Niam was his wife.

But one day, when Usheen was by the beach,
there floated to his feet what seemed a wooden
staff, and he drew it from the waves    It was the
battered fragment of a warrior's lance.  The
blood stains of war were still on it, and as he
looked at it he recalled the old days of the Feni,
the wars and tumult of his youth ; and how he
had outlived his tribe and all had passed away.
Niam came softly to him and rested against his
shoulder, but it did not soothe his pain, and he
heard one of the young men watching him say to
another, " The human sadness has come back
into his eyes."   The people around stood watching him, all sharing his sorrow, and knowing
that his time of happiness was over and that he
would go back among men.  So indeed it was ;
Niam and Usheen mounted the white steed
again and galloped away over the sea, but she
had warned him when they mounted that he

must never dismount for an instant, for that if
he once touched the earth, she and the steed
would vanish forever, that his youth too would
disappear, and that he would be left alone on
earth — an old man whose whole generation had
vanished.

They passed, as before, over the sea; the same
visions hovered around them, youths and maidens
and animals of the chase; they passed by many
islands, and at last reached the shore of Erin
again.  As they travelled over its plains and
among its hills, Oisin looked in vain for his old
companions.  A little people had taken their
place, — small men and women, mounted on
horses as small; — and these people gazed in wonder at the mighty Usheen.  "We have heard,"
they said, "of the hero Finn, and the poets have
written many tales of him and of his people, the
Feni.  We have read in old books that he had a
son Usheen who went away with a fairy maiden;
but he was never seen again, and there is no race
of the Feni left."  Yet refusing to believe this,
and always looking round for the people whom
he had known and loved of old, he thought

within himself that perhaps the Feni were not to be seen because they were hunting fierce wolves by night, as they used to do in his boyhood, and that they were therefore sleeping in the daytime; but again an old man said to him, "The Feni are dead." Then he remembered that it was a hundred years, and that his very race had perished, and he turned with contempt on the little men and their little horses. Three hundred of them as he rode by were trying to lift a vast stone, but they staggered under its weight, and at last fell and lay beneath it; then leaning from his saddle Usheen lifted the stone with one hand and flung it five yards. But with the strain the saddle girth broke, and Usheen came to the ground; the white steed shook himself and neighed, then galloped away, bearing Niam with him, and Usheen lay with all his strength gone from him — a feeble old man. The Island of Youth could only be known by those who dwelt always within it, and those mortals who had once left it could dwell there no more.

# V

## BRAN THE BLESSED

THE mighty king Bran, a being of gigantic size, sat one day on the cliffs of his island in the Atlantic Ocean, near to Hades and the Gates of Night, when he saw ships sailing towards him and sent men to ask what they were. They were a fleet sent by Matholweh, the king of Ireland, who had sent to ask for Branwen, Bran's sister, as his wife. Without moving from his rock Bran bid the monarch land, and sent Branwen back with him as queen.

But there came a time when Branwen was ill-treated at the palace; they sent her into the kitchen and made her cook for the court, and they caused the butcher to come every day (after he had cut up the meat) and give her a blow on the ear. They also drew up all their boats on the shore for three years, that she might not send for her brother. But she reared a starling in the cover of the kneading-trough, taught it to speak, and told it how to find her brother; and then she wrote a letter describing her sorrows and bound it to the bird's wing, and it flew to the island and alighted on Bran's shoulder, "ruffling its feathers" (says the Welsh legend) "so that the letter was seen, and they knew that the bird had been reared in a domestic manner." Then Bran resolved to cross the sea, but he had to wade through the water, as no ship had yet been built large enough to hold him; and he carried all his musicians (pipers) on his shoulders. As he approached the Irish shore, men ran to the king, saying that they had seen a forest on the sea, where there never before had been a tree, and that they had also seen a mountain which moved. Then the king asked Branwen, the queen, what it could be. She answered, "These are the men of the Island of the Mighty, who have come hither to protect me." "What is the forest?" they asked. "The yards and masts of ships." "What mountain is that by the side of the ships?" "It is Bran my brother, coming to the

D

shoal water and rising." "What is the lofty ridge with the lake on each side?" "That is his nose," she said, "and the two lakes are his fierce eyes."

Then the people were terrified: there was yet a river for Bran to pass, and they broke down the bridge which crossed it, but Bran laid himself down and said, "Who will be a chief, let him be a bridge." Then his men laid hurdles on his back, and the whole army crossed over; and that saying of his became afterwards a proverb. Then the Irish resolved, in order to appease the mighty visitor, to build him a house, because he had never before had one that would hold him; and they decided to make the house large enough to contain the two armies, one on each side. They accordingly built this house, and there were a hundred pillars, and the builders treacherously hung a leathern bag on each side of each pillar and put an armed man inside of each, so that they could all rise by night and kill the sleepers. But Bran's brother, who was a suspicious man, asked the builder what was in the first bag. "Meal, good soul," they answered; and he, putting his hand in, felt a man's head and crushed it with his mighty fingers, and so with the next and the next and with the whole two hundred. After this it did not take long to bring on a quarrel between the two armies, and they fought all day.

After this great fight between the men of Ireland and the men of the Isles of the Mighty there were but seven of these last who escaped, besides their king Bran, who was wounded in the foot with a poisoned dart. Then he knew that he should soon die, but he bade the seven men to cut off his head and told them that they must always carry it with them — that it would never decay and would always be able to speak and be pleasant company for them. "A long time will you be on the road," he said. "In Harlech you will feast seven years, the birds of Rhiannon singing to you all the while. And at the Island of Gwales you will dwell for fourscore years, and you may remain there, bearing the head with you uncorrupted, until you open the door that looks towards the mainland; and after you have once opened that door you can stay no longer, but must set forth to London to bury the head, leaving it there to look toward France."

So they went on to Harlech and there stopped to rest, and sat down to eat and drink. And there came three birds, which began singing a certain song, and all the songs they had ever heard were unpleasant compared with it; and the songs seemed to them to be at a great distance from them, over the sea, yet the notes were heard as distinctly as if they were close by; and it is said that at this repast they continued seven years. At the close of this time they went forth to an island in the sea called Gwales. There they found a fair and regal spot overlooking the ocean and a spacious hall built for them. They went into it and found two of its doors open, but the third door, looking toward Cornwall, was closed. "See yonder," said their leader Manawydan; "that is the door we may not open." And that night they regaled themselves and were joyful. And of all they had seen of food laid before them, and of all they had heard said, they remembered nothing; neither of that, nor of any sorrow whatsoever. There they re-

mained fourscore years, unconscious of having
ever spent a time more joyous and mirthful.
And they were not more weary than when first
they came, neither did they, any of them, know
the time they had been there. It was not more
irksome for them to have the head with them,
than if Bran the Blessed had been with them
himself. And because of these fourscore years,
it was called "The Entertaining of the Noble
Head."

One day said Heilwyn the son of Gwyn,
"Evil betide me, if I do not open the door to
know if that is true which is said concerning it."
So he opened the door and looked towards
Cornwall. And when they had looked they
were as conscious of all the evils they had ever
sustained, and of all the friends and companions
they had ever lost, and of all the misery that had
befallen them, as if all had happened in that very
spot; and especially of the fate of their lord.
And because of their perturbation they could not
rest, but journeyed forth with the head towards
London. And they buried the head in the
White Mount.

The island called Gwales is supposed to be that now named Gresholm, eight or ten miles off the coast of Pembrokeshire; and to this day the Welsh sailors on that coast talk of the Green Meadows of Enchantment lying out at sea west of them, and of men who had either landed on them or seen them suddenly vanishing. Some of the people of Milford used to declare that they could sometimes see the Green Islands of the fairies quite distinctly; and they believed that the fairies went to and fro between their islands and the shore through a subterranean gallery under the sea. They used, indeed, to make purchases in the markets of Milford or Langhorne, and this they did sometimes without being seen and always without speaking, for they seemed to know the prices of the things they wished to buy and always laid down the exact sum of money needed. And indeed, how could the seven companions of the Enchanted Head have spent eighty years of incessant feasting on an island of the sea, without sometimes purchasing supplies from the mainland?

# VI

## THE CASTLE OF THE ACTIVE DOOR

> Perfect is my chair in Caer Sidi;
> Plague and age hurt not who's in it —
> They know, Manawydan and Pryderi.
> Three organs round a fire sing before it,
> And about its points are ocean's streams
> And the abundant well above it —
> Sweeter than white wine the drink in it.

PEREDUR, the knight, rode through the wild woods of the Enchanted Island until he arrived on clear ground outside the forest. Then he beheld a castle on level ground in the middle of a meadow; and round the castle flowed a stream, and inside the castle there were large and spacious halls with great windows. Drawing nearer the castle, he saw it to be turning more rapidly than any wind blows. On the ramparts he saw archers shooting so vigorously that no armor would protect against them; there were also men blowing horns so loud that the earth appeared to tremble; and at the gates were lions, in iron chains, roaring so violently that one might fancy that the castle and the woods were ready to be uprooted. Neither the lions nor the warriors resisted Peredur, but he found a woman sitting by the gate, who offered to carry him on her back to the hall. This was the queen Rhiannon, who, having been accused of having caused the death of her child, was sentenced to remain seven years sitting by the gate, to tell her story to every one, and to offer to carry all strangers on her back into the castle.

But so soon as Peredur had entered it, the castle vanished away, and he found himself standing on the bare ground. The queen Rhiannon was left beside him, and she remained on the island with her son Pryderi and his wife. Queen Rhiannon married for her second husband a person named Manawydan. One day they ascended a mound called Arberth which was well known for its wonders, and as they sat there they heard a clap of thunder, followed by mist so thick that they could not see one another. When it grew light again, they looked around them and found that all dwellings and animals had vanished; there was no smoke or fire anywhere or work of human hands; all their household had disappeared, and there were left only Pryderi and Manawydan with their wives. Wandering from place to place, they found no human beings; but they lived by hunting, fishing, and gathering wild honey. After visiting foreign lands, they returned to their island home.

One day when they were out hunting, a wild boar of pure white color sprang from a bush, and as they saw him they retreated, and they saw also the Turning Castle. The boar, watching his opportunity, sprang into it, and the dogs followed, and Pryderi said, " I will go into this castle and get tidings of the dogs." "Go not," said Manawydan; "whoever has cast a spell over this land and deprived us of our dwelling has placed this castle here." But Pryderi replied, "Of a truth I cannot give up my dogs." So he watched for the opportunity and went in. He saw neither boar nor dogs, neither man nor beast; but on the centre of the castle floor he saw a fountain with marble work around it, and on the margin of the fountain a golden bowl upon a marble slab, and in the air hung chains, of which he could see no end.  He was much delighted with the beauty of the gold and the rich workmanship of the bowl and went up to lay hold of it.  The moment he touched it, his fingers clung to the bowl, and his feet to the slab ; and all his joyousness forsook him so that. he could not utter a word.  And thus he stood.

Manawydan waited for him until evening, but hearing nothing either of him or of the dogs, he returned home.  When he entered, Rhiannon, who was his wife and who was also Pryderi's mother, looked at him.  " Where," she said, " are Pryderi and the dogs ? "  " This is what has happened to me," he said ; and he told her. " An evil companion hast thou been," she said, " and a good companion hast thou lost."  With these words she went out and proceeded towards the Castle of the Active Door.  Getting in, she saw Pryderi taking hold of the bowl, and she went towards him.  " What dost thou here ? " she said, and she took hold of the bowl for herself ; and then her hands became fast to it, and

"The hands of Pryderi and Rhiannon were held fast by the enchanted bowl, and their feet by the enchanted slab; and their joyousness forsook them, and they could not utter a word." — p. 42

her feet to the slab, and she could not speak a word. Then came thunder and a fall of mist; thereupon the Castle of the Active Door vanished and never was seen again. Rhiannon and Pryderi also vanished.

When Kigva, the wife of Pryderi, saw this, she sorrowed so that she cared not if she lived or died. No one was left on the island but Manawydan and herself. They wandered away to other lands and sought to earn their living; then they came back to their island, bringing with them one bag of wheat which they planted. It throve and grew, and when the time of harvest came it was most promising, so that Manawydan resolved to reap it on the morrow. At break of day he came back to begin; but found nothing left but straw. Every stalk had been cut close to the ground and carried away. Going to another field, he found it ripe, but on coming in the morning he found but the straw. "Some one has contrived my ruin," he said; "I will watch the third field to see what happens. He who stole the first will come to steal this."

He remained through the evening to watch the

grain, and at midnight he heard loud thunder. He looked and saw coming a host of mice such as no man could number; each mouse took a stalk of the wheat and climbed it, so that it bent to the ground; then each mouse cut off the ear and ran away with it. They all did this, leaving the stalk bare, and there was not a single straw for which there was not a mouse. He struck among them, but could no more fix his sight on any of them, the legend says, than on flies and birds in the air, except one which seemed heavier than the rest, and moved slowly. This one he pursued and caught, put it in his glove and tied it with a string. Taking it home, he showed it to Kigva, and told her that he was going to hang the mouse next day. She advised against it, but he persisted, and on the next morning took the animal to the top of the Mound of Arberth, where he placed two wooden forks in the ground, and set up a small gallows.

While doing this, he saw a clerk coming to him in old, threadbare clothes. It was now seven years since he had seen a human being there, except the friends he had lost and Kigva who survived them. The clerk bade him good day and said he was going back to his country from England, where he had been singing. Then the clerk asked Manawydan what he was doing. "Hanging a thief," said he; and when the clerk saw that it was a mouse, he offered a pound to release it, but Manawydan refused. Then a priest came riding up and offered him three pounds to release the mouse; but this offer was declined. Then he made a noose round the mouse's neck, and while he did this, a bishop's whole retinue came riding towards him. The bishop seemed, like everybody else, to be very desirous of rescuing the mouse; he offered first seven pounds, and then twenty-four, and then added all his horses and equipages; but Manawydan still refused. The bishop finally asked him to name any price he pleased. "The liberation of Rhiannon and Pryderi," he said. "Thou shalt have it," said the bishop. "And the removal of the enchantment," said Manawydan. "That also," said the bishop, "if you will only restore the mouse." "Why?" said the other. "Because," said the bishop, "she is my wife." "Why did she come to me?" asked Manawydan. "To steal," was the reply. "When it was known that you were inhabiting the island, my household came to me, begging me to transform them into mice. The first and second nights they came alone, but the third night my wife and the ladies of the court wished also to accompany them, and I transformed them also; and now you have promised to let her go." "Not so," said the other, "except with a promise that there shall be no more such enchantment practised, and no vengeance on Pryderi and Rhiannon, or on me." This being promised, the bishop said, "Now wilt thou release my wife?" "No, by my faith," said Manawydan, "not till I see Pryderi and Rhiannon free before my eyes." "Here they are coming," said the bishop; and when they had been embraced by Manawydan, he let go the mouse; the bishop touched it with a wand, and it became the most beautiful young woman that ever was seen. "Now look round upon the country," said the bishop, " and see the dwellings and the crops returned," and the enchantment was removed.

"The Land of Illusion and the Realm of Glamour " is the name given by the old romancers to the south-west part of Wales, and to all the islands off the coast. Indeed, it was believed, ever since the days of the Greek writer, Plutarch, that some peculiar magic belonged to these islands; and every great storm that happened among them was supposed to be caused by the death of one of the wondrous enchanters who dwelt in that region. When it was over, the islanders said, "Some one of the mighty has passed away."

# VII

## MERLIN THE ENCHANTER

IN one of the old books called Welsh Triads, in which all things are classed by threes, there is a description of three men called "The Three Generous Heroes of the Isle of Britain." One of these — named Nud or Nodens, and later called Merlin — was first brought from the sea, it is stated, with a herd of cattle consisting of 21,000 milch cows, which are supposed to mean those waves of the sea that the poets often describe as White Horses. He grew up to be a king and warrior, a magician and prophet, and on the whole the most important figure in the Celtic traditions. He came from the sea and at last returned to it, but meanwhile he did great works on land, one of which is said to have been the building of Stonehenge.

This is the way, as the old legends tell, in which the vast stones of Stonehenge came to

be placed on Salisbury Plain. It is a thing
which has always been a puzzle to every one,
inasmuch as their size and weight are enormous, and there is no stone of the same description to be found within hundreds of miles
of Salisbury Plain, where they now stand.

The legend is that Pendragon, king of England, was led to fight a great battle by seeing a
dragon in the air. The battle was won, but Pendragon was killed and was buried on Salisbury
Plain, where the fight had taken place. When
his brother Uther took his place, Merlin the
enchanter advised him to paint a dragon on a
flag and bear it always before him to bring
good fortune, and this he always did. Then
Merlin said to him, "Wilt thou do nothing
more on the Plain of Salisbury, to honor thy
brother?" The King said, "What shall be
done?" Then Merlin said, "I will cause a
thing to be done that will endure to the
world's end." Then he bade Utherpendragon,
as he called the new king, to send many ships
and men to Ireland, and he showed him stones
such as seemed far too large and heavy to

E

bring, but he placed them by his magic art
upon the boats and bore them to England;
and he devised means to transport them and
to set them on end, "for they shall seem fairer
so than if they were lying." And there they
are to this day.

This was the way in which Merlin would
sometimes obtain the favor and admiration of
young ladies. There was a maiden of twelve
named Nimiane or Vivian, the daughter of
King Dionas, and Merlin changed himself into
the appearance of "a fair young squire," that
he might talk with her beside a fountain, described in the legends as "a well, whereof the
springs were fair and the water clear and the
gravel so fair that it seemed of fine silver." By
degrees he made acquaintance with the child,
who told him who she was, adding, "And what
are you, fair, sweet friend?" "Damsel," said
Merlin, "I am a travelling squire, seeking for
my master, who has taught me wonderful things."
"And what master is that?" she asked. "It
is one," he said, "who has taught me so
much that I could here erect for you a castle,

" Merlin, changed into the appearance of a fair young squire, by degrees made
acquaintance with Vivian, who told him who she was." — p. 50

and I could make many people outside to attack
it and inside to defend it; nay, I could go
upon this water and not wet my feet, and
I could make a river where water had never
been."

"These are strange feats," said the maiden,
"and I wish that I could thus disport myself."
"I can do yet greater things," said Merlin,
"and no one can devise anything which I cannot
do, and I can also make it to endure forever."
"Indeed," said the girl, "I would always love
you if you could show me some such wonders."
"For your love," he answered, "I will show you
some of these wondrous plays, and I will ask no
more of you." Then Merlin turned and described a circle with a wand and then came and
sat by her again at the fountain. At noon she
saw coming out of the forest many ladies and
knights and squires, holding each other by the
hand and singing in the greatest joy; then came
men with timbrels and tabours and dancing, so
that one could not tell one-fourth part of the
sports that went on. Then Merlin caused an
orchard to grow, with all manner of fruit and

flowers; and the maiden cared for nothing but
to listen to their singing, "Truly love begins in
joy, but ends in grief." The festival continued
from mid-day to even-song; and King Dionas
and his courtiers came out to see it, and marvelled whence these strange people came. Then
when the carols were ended, the ladies and
maidens sat down on the green grass and fresh
flowers, and the squires set up a game of tilting
called quintain upon the meadows and played
till even-song; and then Merlin came to the
damsel and asked if he had done what he
promised for her. "Fair, sweet friend," said
she, "you have done so much that I am all
yours." "Let me teach you," he answered,
"and I will show you many wonders that no
woman ever learned so many."

Merlin and this young damsel always remained friends, and he taught her many wonderful arts, one of which was (this we must regret)
a spell by which she might put her parents to
sleep whenever he visited her; while another
lesson was (this being more unexceptionable) in
the use of three words, by saying which she

might at any time keep at a distance any men who tried to molest her. He stayed eight days near her, and in those days taught her many of the most "wonderful things that any mortal heart could think of, things past and things that were done and said, and a part of what was to come; and she put them in writing, and then Merlin departed from her and came to Benoyk, where the king, Arthur, rested, so that glad were they when they saw Merlin."

The relations between Merlin and Arthur are unlike those ever held towards a king even by an enchanter in any legend. Even in Homer there is no one described, except the gods, as having such authority over a ruler. Merlin came and went as he pleased and under any form he might please. He foretold the result of a battle, ordered up troops, brought aid from a distance. He rebuked the bravest knights for cowardice; as when Ban, Bors, and Gawain had concealed themselves behind some bushes during a fight. "Is this," he said to King Arthur and Sir Bors, "the war and the help that you do to your friends who have put themselves in adventure of death in many a need, and ye come hither to hide for cowardice." Then the legend says, "When the king understood the words of Merlin, he bowed his head for shame," and the other knights acknowledged their fault. Then Merlin took the dragon banner which he had given them and said that he would bear it himself; "for the banner of a king," he said, "should not be hid in battle, — but borne in the foremost front." Then Merlin rode forth and cried with a loud voice, "Now shall be shown who is a knight." And the knights, seeing Merlin, exclaimed that he was "a full noble man"; and "without fail," says the legend, "he was full of marvellous powers and strength of body and great and long stature; but brown he was and lean and rough of hair." Then he rode in among the enemy on a great black horse; and the golden dragon which he had made and had attached to the banner gave out from its throat such a flaming fire that the air was black with its smoke; and all King Arthur's men began to fight again more stoutly, and Arthur himself held the bridle reins in his left hand, and so wielded his sword with his right as to slay two hundred men.

There was no end to Merlin's disguises — sometimes as an old man, sometimes as a boy or a dwarf, then as a woman, then as an ignorant clown; — but the legends always give him some object to accomplish, some work to do, and there was always a certain dignity about him, even when helping King Arthur, as he sometimes did, to do wrong things. His fame extended over all Britain, and also through Brittany, now a part of France, where the same poetic legends extended. This, for instance, is a very old Breton song about him: —

### MERLIN THE DIVINER

Merlin! Merlin! where art thou going
So early in the day, with thy black dog?
Oi! oi! oi! oi! oi! oi! oi! oi! oi! oi! oi!
Oi! oi! oi! ioi! oi!

I have come here to search the way,
To find the red egg;
The red egg of the marine serpent,
By the seaside, in the hollow of the stone.

I am going to seek in the valley
The green water-cress, and the golden grass,
And the top branch of the oak,
In the wood by the side of the fountain.

Merlin ! Merlin ! retrace your steps ;
Leave the branch on the oak,
And the green water-cress in the valley,
As well as the golden grass ;
And leave the red egg of the marine serpent
In the foam by the hollow of the stone.
Merlin ! Merlin ! retrace thy steps ;
There is no diviner but God.

Merlin was supposed to know the past, the present, and the future, and to be able to assume the form of any animal, and even that of a *menhir*, or huge standing stone. Before history began he ruled in Britain, then a delightful island of flowery meadows. His subjects were "small people" (fairies), and their lives were a continued festival of singing, playing, and enjoyment. The sage ruled them as a father, his familiar servant being a tame wolf. He also possessed a kingdom, beneath the waves, where everything was beautiful, the

inhabitants being charming little beings, with
waves of long, fair hair falling on their shoulders in curls. Fruits and milk composed the
food of all, meat and fish being held in abhor-
rence. The only want felt was of the full light
of the sun, which, coming to them through the
water, was but faint, and cast no shadow.

Here was the famous workshop where Merlin forged the enchanted sword so celebrated
by the bards, and where the stones were found
by which alone the sword could be sharpened.
Three British heroes were fated to wield this
blade in turn; viz., Lemenisk the leaper
(*Leim*, meaning leap), Utherpendragon, and his
son King Arthur. By orders of this last hero,
when mortally wounded, it was flung into the
sea, where it will remain till he returns to
restore the rule of his country to the faithful
British race.

The bard once amused and puzzled the court
by entering the hall as a blind boy led by a
greyhound, playing on his harp, and demand-
ing as recompense to be allowed to carry the
king's banner in an approaching battle. Being

refused on account of his blindness he vanished, and the king of Brittany mentioned his suspicions that this was one of Merlin's elfin tricks. Arthur was disturbed, for he had promised to give the child anything except his honor, his kingdom, his wife, and his sword. However, while he continued to fret, there entered the hall a poor child about eight years old, with shaved head, features of livid tint, eyes of light gray, barefooted, barelegged, and a whip knotted over his shoulders in the manner affected by horse-boys. Speaking and looking like an idiot, he asked the king's permission to bear the royal ensign in the approaching battle with the giant Rion. The courtiers laughed, but Arthur, suspecting a new joke on Merlin's part, granted the demand, and then Merlin stood in his own proper person before the company.

He also seems to have taught people many things in real science, especially the women, who were in those days more studious than the men, or at least had less leisure. For instance, the legend says of Morgan le fay (or la fée), King Arthur's sister, "she was a noble clergesse (meaning that she could read and write, like the clergy), and of astronomy could she enough, for Merlin had her taught, and she learned much of egromancy (magic or necromancy); and the best work-woman she was with her hands that any man knew in any land, and she had the fairest head and the fairest hands under heaven, and shoulders well-shapen; and she had fair eloquence and full debonair she was, as long as she was in her right wit; and when she was wroth with any man, she was evil to meet." This lady was one of Merlin's pupils, but the one whom he loved most and instructed the most was Nimiane or Vivian, already mentioned, who seems to have been to him rather a beloved younger sister than anything else, and he taught her so much that "at last he might hold himself a fool," the legend says, "and ever she inquired of his cunning and his mysteries, each thing by itself, and he let her know all, and she wrote all that he said, as she was well learned in clergie (reading and writing), and learned lightly all that Merlin taught her; and when they parted, each of them commended the other to God full tenderly."

The form of the enchanter Merlin disappeared from view, at last — for the legends do not admit that his life ever ended — across the sea whence he came.

The poet Tennyson, to be sure, describes Nimiane or Vivian — the Lady of the Lake — as a wicked enchantress who persuaded Merlin to betray his secrets to her, and then shut him up in an oak tree forever. But other legends seem to show that Tennyson does great injustice to the Lady of the Lake, that she really loved Merlin even in his age, and therefore persuaded him to show her how to make a tower without walls, — that they might dwell there together in peace, and address each other only as Brother and Sister. When he had told her, he fell asleep with his head in her lap, and she wove a spell nine times around his head, and the tower became the strongest in the world. Some of the many legends place this tower in the forest of Broceliande; while others transport it afar to a magic island, where Merlin dwells with his nine bards, and where Vivian alone can come or go through the magic walls. Some legends describe it as an enclosure " neither of iron nor steel nor timber nor of stone, but of the air, without any other thing but enchantment, so strong that it may never be undone while the world endureth." Here dwells Merlin, it is said, with nine favorite bards who took with them the thirteen treasures of England. These treasures are said to have been : —

1. A sword; if any man drew it except the owner, it burst into a flame from the cross to the point. All who asked it received it; but because of this peculiarity all shunned it.

2. A basket; if food for one man were put into it, when opened it would be found to contain food for one hundred.

3. A horn; what liquor soever was desired was found therein.

4. A chariot; whoever sat in it would be immediately wheresoever he wished.

5. A halter, which was in a staple below the feet of a bed; and whatever horse one wished for in it, he would find it there.

6. A knife, which would serve four-and-twenty men at meat all at once.

7. A caldron; if meat were put into it to boil for a coward, it would never be boiled; but if meat were put in it for a brave man, it would be boiled forthwith.

8. A whetstone; if the sword of a brave man were sharpened thereon, and any one were wounded therewith, he would be sure to die; but if it were that of a coward that was sharpened on it, he would be none the worse.

9. A garment; if a man of gentle birth put it on, it suited him well; but if a churl, it would not fit him.

10, 11. A pan and a platter; whatever food was required was found therein.

12. A chessboard; when the men were placed upon it, they would play of themselves. The chessboard was of gold, and the men of silver.

13. The mantle of Arthur; whosoever was beneath it could see everything, while no one could see him.

It is towards this tower, some legends say, that Merlin was last seen by some Irish monks, sailing away westward, with a maiden, in a boat of crystal, beneath a sunset sky.

# VIII

## SIR LANCELOT OF THE LAKE

SIR LANCELOT, the famous knight, was the son of a king and queen against whom their subjects rebelled; the king was killed, the queen taken captive, when a fairy rose in a cloud of mist and carried away the infant Lancelot from where he had been left beneath a tree. The queen, after weeping on the body of her husband, looked round and saw a lady standing by the water-side, holding the queen's child in her arms. "Fair, sweet friend," said the queen, "give me back my child." The fairy made no reply, but dived into the water; and the queen was taken to an abbey, where she was known as the Queen of Great Griefs. The Lady of the Lake took the child to her own home, which was an island in the middle of the sea and surrounded by impassable walls. From this the lady had her

name of Dame du Lac, or the Lady of the
Lake (or Sea), and her foster son was called
Lancelot du Lac, while the realm was called
Meidelant, or the Land of Maidens.

Lancelot dwelt thenceforward in the castle,
on the island. When he was eight years old
he received a tutor who was to instruct him in
all knightly knowledge; he learned to use bow
and spear and to ride on horseback, and some
cousins of his were also brought thither by the
Lady of the Lake to be his comrades. When
he was eighteen he wished to go to King
Arthur's court that he might be a knight.

On the eve of St. John, as King Arthur returned from the chase, and by the high road
approached Camelot, he met a fair company.
In the van went two youths, leading two white
mules, one freighted with a silken pavilion, the
other with robes proper for a newly made knight;
the mules bore two chests, holding the hauberk
and the iron boots. Next came two squires,
clad in white robes and mounted on white
horses, carrying a silver shield and a shining
helmet; after these, two others, with a sword

in a white sheath and a white charger. Behind
followed squires and servants in white coats,
three damsels dressed in white, the two sons
of King Bors; and, last of all, the fairy with
the youth she loved. Her robe was of white
samite lined with ermine; her white palfrey
had a silver bit, while her breastplate, stirrups,
and saddle were of ivory, carved with figures
of ladies and knights, and her white housings
trailed on the ground.

When she perceived the king, she responded
to his salutation, and said, after she had lowered her wimple and displayed her face: "Sir,
may God bless the best of kings! I come to
implore a boon, which it shall cost you nothing to grant." "Damsel, even it should cost
me dear, you should not be refused; what is it
you would have me do?" "Sir, dub this
varlet a knight, and array him in the arms
he bringeth, whenever he desireth." "Your
mercy, damsel! to bring me such a youth!
Assuredly, I will dub him whenever he will;
but it shameth me to abandon my custom,
for 'tis my wont to furnish with garments and

F

arms such as come thither to receive chivalry."
The lady replied that she desired the youth
to carry the arms she had intended him to
wear, and if she were refused, she would address herself elsewhere.  Sir Ewain said that so
fair a youth ought not to be denied, and the
king yielded to her entreaty.  She returned
thanks, and bade the varlet retain the mules
and the charger, with the two squires; and after
that, she prepared to return as she had come,
in spite of the urgency of the king, who had
begged her to remain in his court.  "At least,"
he cried, "tell us by what name are you
known?"  "Sir," she answered, "I am called
the Lady of the Lake."

For a long way, Lancelot escorted the fairy,
who said to him as she took leave: "King's
son, you are derived from lineage the most
noble on earth; see to it that your worth be
as great as your beauty.  To-morrow you will
ask the king to bestow on you knighthood;
when you are armed, you will not tarry in his
house a single night.  Abide in one place no
longer than you can help, and refrain from

declaring your name until others proclaim it. Be prepared to accomplish every adventure, and never let another man complete a task which you yourself have undertaken." With that, she gave him a ring that had the property of dissolving enchantment, and commended him to God.

On the morrow, Lancelot arrayed himself in his fairest robes, and sued for knighthood, as he had been commanded to do. Sir Ewain attended him to court, where they dismounted in front of the palace; the king and queen advanced to meet them; each took Sir Ewain by a hand, and seated him on a couch, while the varlet stood in their presence on the rushes that strewed the floor. All gazed with pleasure, and the queen prayed that God might make him noble, for he possessed as much beauty as was possible for man to have.

After this he had many perilous adventures; he fought with giants and lions; he entered an enchanted castle and escaped; he went to a well in the forest, and, striking three times on a cymbal with a hammer hung there for the purpose, called forth a great giant, whom he slew, afterwards marrying his daughter. Then he went to rescue the queen of the realm, Gwenivere, from captivity. In order to reach the fortress where she was prisoner, he had to ride in a cart with a dwarf; to follow a wheel that rolled before him to show him the way, or a ball that took the place of the wheel; he had to walk on his hands and knees across a bridge made of a drawn sword; he suffered greatly. At last he rescued the queen, and later than this he married Elaine, the daughter of King Pelles, and her father gave to them the castle of Blyaunt in the Joyous Island, enclosed in iron, and with a deep water all around it. There Lancelot challenged all knights to come and contend with him, and he jousted with more than five hundred, overcoming them all, yet killing none, and at last he returned to Camelot, the place of King Arthur's court.

One day he was called from the court to an abbey, where three nuns brought to him a beautiful boy of fifteen, asking that he might be made a knight. This was Sir Lancelot's own son, Galahad, whom he had never seen, and did not yet know. That evening Sir Lancelot remained at the abbey with the boy, that he might keep his vigil there, and on the morrow's dawn he was made a knight. Sir Lancelot put on one of his spurs, and Bors, Lancelot's cousin, the other, and then Sir Lancelot said to the boy, "Fair son, attend me to the court of the king;" but the abbess said, "Sir, not now, but we will send him when it shall be time."

On Whitsunday, at the time called "underne," which was nine in the morning, King Arthur and his knights sat at the Round Table, where on every seat there was written, in letters of gold, the name of a knight with "here ought to sit he," or "he ought to sit here;" and thus went the inscriptions until they came to one seat (or *siège* in French) called the "Siege Perilous," where they found newly written letters of gold, saying that this seat could not be occupied until four hundred and fifty years after the death of Christ; and that was this very day. Then there came news

of a marvellous stone which had been seen
above the water, with a sword sticking in it
bearing the letters, " Never shall man take
me hence, but only he by whose side I ought
to hang, and he shall be the best knight of
the world." Then two of the knights tried
to draw the sword and failed to draw it, and
Sir Lancelot, who was thought the best knight
in all the world, refused to attempt it. Then
they went back to their seats around the table.

Then when all the seats but the " Siege
Perilous " were full, the hall was suddenly
darkened ; and an old man clad in white, whom
nobody knew, came in, with a young knight in
red armor, wearing an empty scabbard at his side,
who said, " Peace be with you, fair knights."
The old man said, "I bring you here a young
knight that is of kings' lineage," and the king
said, " Sir, ye are right heartily welcome."
Then the old man bade the young knight to
remove his armor, and he wore a red garment,
while the old man placed on his shoulders a
mantle of fine ermine, and said, " Sir, follow
after." Then the old man led him to the " Siege

Perilous," next to Sir Lancelot, and lifted the cloth and read, "Here sits Sir Galahad," and the youth sat down. Upon this, all the knights of the Round Table marvelled greatly at Sir Galahad, that he dared to sit in that seat, and he so tender of age. Then King Arthur took him by the hand and led him down to the river to see the adventure of the stone. "Sir," said the king to Sir Galahad, "here is a great marvel, where right good knights have tried and failed." "Sir," said Sir Galahad, "that is no marvel, for the adventure was not theirs, but mine; I have brought no sword with me, for here by my side hangs the scabbard," and he laid his hand on the sword and lightly drew it from the stone.

It was not until long after, and when they both had had many adventures, that Sir Lancelot discovered Galahad to be his son. Sir Lancelot once came to the sea-strand and found a ship without sails or oars, and sailed away upon it. Once, when he touched at an island, a young knight came on board to whom Lancelot said, "Sir, you are welcome," and when the young

knight asked his name, told him, " My name is
Sir Lancelot du Lac." " Sir," he said, " then
you are welcome, for you are my father." "Ah,"
said Lancelot, "are you Sir Galahad ? " Then
the young knight kneeled down and asked his
blessing, and they embraced each other, and there
was great joy between them, and they told each
other all their deeds. So dwelt Sir Lancelot
and Sir Galahad together within that ship for
half a year, and often they arrived at islands far
from men where there were but wild beasts,
and they found many adventures strange and
perilous which they brought to an end.

When Sir Lancelot at last died, his body was
taken to Joyous-Gard, his home, and there it
lay in state in the choir, with a hundred torches
blazing above it ; and while it was there, came
his brother Sir Ector de Maris, who had long
been seeking Lancelot. When he heard such
noise and saw such lights in the choir, he alighted
and came in ; and Sir Bors went towards him and
told him that his brother Lancelot was lying
dead. Then Sir Ector threw his shield and
sword and helm from him, and when he looked

on Sir Lancelot's face he fell down in a swoon, and when he rose he spoke thus: "Ah, Sir Lancelot," said he, "thou wert dead of all Christen knights! And now I dare say, that, Sir Lancelot, there thou liest, thou wert never matched of none earthly knight's hands; and thou wert the curtiest knight that ever beare shield; and thou wert the truest friend to thy lover that ever bestrood horse, and thou wert the truest lover of a sinful man that ever loved woman; and thou wert the kindest man that ever strooke with sword; and thou wert the goodliest person that ever came among presse of knights; and thou wert the meekest man and the gentlest that ever eate in hall among ladies; and thou wert the sternest knight to thy mortall foe that ever put speare in the rest."

# IX

## THE HALF-MAN

KING ARTHUR in his youth was fond of all manly exercises, especially of wrestling, an art in which he found few equals. The old men who had been the champions of earlier days, and who still sat, in summer evenings, watching the youths who tried their skill before them, at last told him that he had no rival in Cornwall, and that his only remaining competitor elsewhere was one who had tired out all others.

" Where is he ? " said Arthur.

" He dwells," an old man said, " on an island whither you will have to go and find him. He is of all wrestlers the most formidable. You will think him at first so insignificant as to be hardly worth a contest; you will easily throw him at the first trial; but after a while you will find him growing stronger; he seeks out all

your weak points as by magic; he never gives
up; you may throw him again and again, but he
will conquer you at last."

" His name ! his name ! " said Arthur.

" His name," they answered, " is Hanner
Dyn; his home is everywhere, but on his own
island you will be likely to find him sooner or
later. Keep clear of him, or he will get the best
of you in the end, and make you his slave as
he makes slaves of others whom he has conquered."

Far and wide over the ocean the young
Arthur sought; he touched at island after
island; he saw many weak men who did not
dare to wrestle with him, and many strong ones
whom he could always throw, until at last when
he was far out under the western sky, he came
one day to an island which he had never before
seen and which seemed uninhabited. Presently
there came out from beneath an arbor of flowers
a little miniature man, graceful and quick-mov-
ing as an elf. Arthur, eager in his quest, said
to him, " In what island dwells Hanner Dyn ? "
" In this island," was the answer. " Where is

he?" said Arthur. "I am he," said the laughing boy, taking hold of his hand.

"What did they mean by calling you a wrestler?" said Arthur.

"Oh," said the child coaxingly, "I am a wrestler. Try me."

The king took him and tossed him in the air with his strong arms, till the boy shouted with delight. He then took Arthur by the hand and led him about the island — showed him his house and where the gardens and fields were. He showed him the rows of men toiling in the meadows or felling trees. "They all work for me," he said carelessly. The king thought he had never seen a more stalwart set of laborers. Then the boy led him to the house, asked him what his favorite fruits were, or his favorite beverages, and seemed to have all at hand. He was an unaccountable little creature; in size and years he seemed a child; but in his activity and agility he seemed almost a man. When the king told him so, he smiled, as winningly as ever, and said, "That is what they call me — Hanner Dyn, The Half-Man." Laughing merrily, he helped Arthur into his boat and bade him farewell, urging him to come again. The King sailed away, looking back with something like affection on his winsome little playmate.

It was months before Arthur came that way again. Again the merry child met him, having grown a good deal since their earlier meeting. "How is my little wrestler?" said Arthur. "Try me," said the boy; and the king tossed him again in his arms, finding the delicate limbs firmer, and the slender body heavier than before, though easily manageable. The island was as green and more cultivated, there were more men working in the fields, and Arthur noticed that their look was not cheerful, but rather as of those who had been discouraged and oppressed.

It was, however, a charming sail to the island, and, as it became more familiar, the king often bade his steersman guide the pinnace that way. He was often startled with the rapid growth and increased strength of the laughing boy, Hanner Dyn, while at other times he seemed much as before and appeared to have made but little progress. The youth seemed never tired of wrestling; he always begged the king for a trial of skill, and the king rejoiced to see how readily the young wrestler caught at the tricks of the art ; so that the time had long passed when even Arthur's strength could toss him lightly in the air, as at first. Hanner Dyn was growing with incredible rapidity into a tall young fellow, and instead of the weakness that often comes with rapid growth, his muscles grew ever harder and harder. Still merry and smiling, he began to wrestle in earnest, and one day, in a moment of carelessness, Arthur received a back fall, perhaps on moist ground, and measured his length. Rising with a quick motion, he laughed at the angry faces of his attendants and bade the boy farewell. The men at work in the fields glanced up, attracted by the sound of voices, and he saw them exchange looks with one another.

Yet he felt his kingly dignity a little impaired, and hastened ere long to revisit the island and teach the saucy boy another lesson. Months had passed, and the youth had expanded into a man of princely promise, but with the same sunny look. His shoulders were now broad, his limbs of the firmest mould, his eye clear, keen, penetrating. "Of all the wrestlers I have ever yet met," said the king, "this younker promises to be the most formidable. I can easily throw him now, but what will he be a few years hence?" The youth greeted him joyously, and they began their usual match. The sullen serfs in the fields stopped to watch them, and an aged Druid priest, whom Arthur had brought with him, to give the old man air and exercise in the boat, opened his weak eyes and closed them again.

As they began to wrestle, the king felt, by the very grasp of the youth's arms, by the firm set of his foot upon the turf, that this was to be unlike any previous effort. The wrestlers stood after the old Cornish fashion, breast to breast, each resting his chin on the other's shoulder. They grasped each other round the body, each setting his left hand above the other's right. Each tried to force the other to touch the ground with both shoulders and one hip, or with both hips and one shoulder;

or else to compel the other to relinquish his hold for an instant — either of these successes giving the victory. Often as Arthur had tried the art, he never had been so matched before. The competitors swayed this way and that, writhed, struggled, half lost their footing and regained it, yet neither yielded. All the boatmen gathered breathlessly around, King Arthur's men refusing to believe their eyes, even when they knew their king was in danger. A stranger group was that of the sullen farm-laborers, who left their ploughs and spades, and, congregating on a rising ground, watched without any expression of sympathy the contest that was going on. An old wrestler from Cornwall, whom Arthur had brought with him, was the judge; and according to the habit of the time, the contest was for the best two bouts in three. By the utmost skill and strength, Arthur compelled Hanner Dyn to lose his hold for one instant in the first trial, and the King was pronounced the victor.

The second test was far more difficult; the boy, now grown to a man, and seeming to grow

older and stronger before their very eyes, twice
forced Arthur to the ground either with hip or
shoulder, but never with both, while the crowd
closed in breathlessly around; and the half-
blind old Druid, who had himself been a wrestler in his youth, and who had been brought
ashore to witness the contest, called warningly
aloud, "Save thyself, O king!" At this
Arthur roused his failing strength to one final
effort, and, griping his rival round the waist
with a mighty grasp, raised him bodily from
the ground and threw him backward till he
fell flat, like a log, on both shoulders and both
hips; while Arthur himself fell fainting a
moment later. Nor did he recover until he
found himself in the boat, his head resting on
the knees of the aged Druid, who said to him,
"Never again, O king! must you encounter
the danger you have barely escaped. Had you
failed, you would have become subject to your
opponent, whose strength has been maturing
for years to overpower you. Had you yielded,
you would, although a king, have become but
as are those dark-browed men who till his

G

fields and do his bidding. For know you not what the name Hanner Dyn means? It means — Habit; and the force of habit, at first weak, then growing constantly stronger, ends in conquering even kings!"

# X

## KING ARTHUR AT AVALON

IN the ruined castle at Winchester, England, built by William the Conqueror, there is a hall called "The Great Hall," where Richard Cœur de Lion was received by his nobles when rescued from captivity; where Henry III. was born; where all the Edwards held court; where Henry VIII. entertained the emperor Charles V.; where Queen Mary was married to Philip II.; where Parliament met for many years. It is now a public hall for the county; and at one end of it the visitor sees against the wall a vast wooden tablet on which the names of King Arthur's knights of the Round Table are inscribed in a circle. No one knows its date or origin, though it is known to be more than four hundred years old, but there appear upon it the names most familiar to those who have read the legends of

King Arthur, whether in Tennyson's poems
or elsewhere.   There are Lancelot and Bedivere, Gawaine and Dagonet, Modred and
Gareth, and the rest.   Many books have been
written of their deeds; but a time came when
almost all those knights were to fall, according
to the legend, in one great battle.   Modred,
the king's nephew, had been left in charge of
the kingdom during Arthur's absence, and had
betrayed him and tried to dethrone him, meaning to crown himself king.   Many people
joined with him, saying that under Arthur they
had had only war and fighting, but under
Modred they would have peace and bliss.   Yet
nothing was farther from Modred's purpose
than bliss or peace, and it was agreed at last·
that a great battle should be fought for the
kingdom.

On the night of Trinity Sunday, King
Arthur had a dream.   He thought he sat in a
chair, upon a scaffold, and the chair was
fastened to a wheel.   He was dressed in the
richest cloth of gold that could be made, but
far beneath him he saw a pit, full of black

" And the chair was fastened to a wheel, and the wheel began to turn, and King
Arthur went down, down among the floating things, and they wreathed themselves about him till he cried, ' Help ! help ! ' " — p. 85

water, in which were all manner of serpents
and floating beasts. Then the wheel began to
turn, and he went down, down among the floating things, and they wreathed themselves about
him till he cried, "Help! help!"

Then his knights and squires and yeomen
aroused him, but he slumbered again, not sleeping nor thoroughly waking. Then he thought
he saw his nephew, Sir Gawaine, with a number of fair ladies, and when King Arthur saw
him, he said, "O fair nephew, what are these
ladies who come with you?" "Sir," said Sir
Gawaine, "these are the ladies for whose protection I fought while I was a living man, and
God has given them grace that they should
bring me thither to you, to warn you of your
death. If you fight with Sir Modred to-morrow, you must be slain, and most of your
people on both sides." So Sir Gawaine and
all the ladies vanished, and then the king
called upon his knights and squires and yeomen, and summoned his lords and bishops.
They agreed to propose to Sir Modred that
they should have a month's delay, and mean-

while agreed to meet him with fourteen persons
on each side, besides Arthur and Modred.

Each of these leaders warned his army, when
they met, to watch the other, and not to draw
their swords until they saw a drawn sword on
the other side. In that case they were to come
on fiercely. So the small party of chosen men
on each side met and drank wine together,
and agreed upon a month's delay before fighting; but while this was going on an adder
came out of a bush and stung a knight on the
foot, and he drew his sword to slay it and
thought of nothing farther. At the sight of
that sword the two armies were in motion,
trumpets were blown instantly, and the men
of each army thought that the other army had
begun the fray. "Alas, this unhappy day!"
cried King Arthur; and, as the old chronicle
says, "nothing there was but rushing and riding, fencing and striking, and many a grim
word was there spoken either to other, and
many a deadly stroke."

The following is the oldest account of the
battle, translated into quaint and literal English

by Madden from the book called "Layamon's Brut": "Innumerable folk it came toward the host, riding and on foot, as the rain down falleth! Arthur marched to Cornwall, with an immense army. Modred heard that, and advanced against him with innumerable folk, — there were many fated! Upon the Tambre they came together; the place hight Camelford, evermore lasted the same word. And at Camelford was assembled sixty thousand, and more thousands thereto; Modred was their chief. Then thitherward 'gan ride Arthur the mighty, with innumerable folk, — fated though it were! Upon the Tambre they encountered together; elevated their standards; advanced together; drew their long swords; smote on the helms; fire outsprang; spears splintered; shields 'gan shiver; shafts brake in pieces. There fought all together innumerable folk! Tambre was in flood with blood to excess; there might no man in the fight know any warrior, nor who did worse, nor who better, so was the conflict mingled! For each slew downright, were he swain, were he knight.

There was Modred slain, and deprived of life-
day, and all his knights slain in the fight.
There were slain all the brave, Arthur's warriors, high and low, and all the Britons of
Arthur's board, and all his dependents, of
many kingdoms.    And Arthur wounded with
broad slaughter-spear; fifteen dreadful wounds
he had; in the least one might thrust two
gloves!  Then was there no more remained
in the fight, of two hundred thousand men that
there lay hewed in pieces, except Arthur the
king alone, and two of his knights.    Arthur
was wounded wondrously much.  There came
to him a lad, who was of his kindred; he was
Cador's son, the earl of Cornwall; Constantine
the lad hight, he was dear to the king.  Arthur
looked on him, where he lay on the ground,
and said these words, with sorrowful heart:
'Constantine, thou art welcome; thou wert
Cador's son.  I give thee here my kingdom,
and defend thou my Britons ever in thy life,
and maintain them all the laws that have stood
in my days, and all the good laws that in
Uther's days stood.  And I will fare to Ava-

lon, to the fairest of all maidens, to Argante the queen, an elf most fair, and she shall make my wounds all sound, make me all whole with healing draughts. And afterwards I will come to my kingdom, and dwell with the Britons with mickle joy.' Even with the words there approached from the sea that was a short boat, floating with the waves; and two women therein, wondrously formed; and they took Arthur anon, and bare him quickly, and laid him softly down, and forth they 'gan depart. Then was it accomplished that Merlin whilom said, that mickle care should be of Arthur's departure. The Britons believe yet that he is alive, and dwelleth in Avalon with the fairest of all elves; and the Britons ever yet expect when Arthur shall return. Was never the man born, of any lady chosen, that knoweth, of the sooth, to say more of Arthur. But whilom was a sage hight Merlin; he said with words, —his sayings were sooth,—that an Arthur should yet come to help the English."

Another traditional account which Tennyson has mainly followed in a poem, is this: The king bade Sir Bedivere take his good sword Excalibur and go with it to the water-side and throw it into the water and return to tell what he saw. Then Sir Bedivere took the sword, and it was so richly and preciously adorned that he would not throw it, and came back without it. When the king asked what had happened, Sir Bedivere said, "I saw nothing but waves and wind," and when Arthur did not believe him, and sent him again, he made the same answer, and then, when sent a third time, he threw the sword into the water, as far as he could. Then an arm and a hand rose above the water and caught it, and shook and brandished it three times and vanished.

Then Sir Bedivere came back to the king; he told what he had seen. "Alas," said Arthur, "help me from hence, for I fear I have tarried over long." Then Sir Bedivere took King Arthur upon his back, and went with him to the water's side. And when they had reached there, a barge with many fair ladies was lying there, with many ladies in it, and among them three queens, and they all had

black hoods, and they wept and shrieked when
they saw King Arthur.

"Now put me in the barge," said Arthur,
and the three queens received him with great
tenderness, and King Arthur laid his head in
the lap of one, and she said, "Ah, dear brother,
why have ye tarried so long, until your wound
was cold?" And then they rowed away, and
King Arthur said to Sir Bedivere, "I will go
unto the valley of Avalon to heal my grievous
wound, and if I never return, pray for my soul."
He was rowed away by the weeping queens,
and one of them was Arthur's sister Morgan
le Fay; another was the queen of Northgalis,
and the third was the queen of Waste Lands;
and it was the belief for years in many parts
of England that Arthur was not dead, but
would come again to reign in England, when
he had been nursed long enough by Morgan
le Fay in the island of Avalon.

The tradition was that King Arthur lived
upon this island in an enchanted castle which
had the power of a magnet, so that every one
who came near it was drawn thither and could

not get away. Morgan le Fay was its ruler
(called more correctly Morgan la fée, or the
fairy), and her name Morgan meant sea-born.
By one tradition, the queens who bore away
Arthur were accompanied in the boat by the
bard and enchanter, Merlin, who had long been
the king's adviser, and this is the description
of the island said to have been given by Merlin
to another bard, Taliessin: —

"'We came to that green and fertile island
which each year is blessed with two autumns,
two springs, two summers, two gatherings of
fruit, — the land where pearls are found, where
the flowers spring as you gather them — that
isle of orchards called the "Isle of the Blessed."
No tillage there, no coulter to tear the bosom
of the earth. Without labor it affords wheat
and the grape. There the lives extend beyond
a century. There nine sisters, whose will is
the only law, rule over those who go from us
to them. The eldest excels in the art of healing, and exceeds her sisters in beauty. She is
called Morgana, and knows the virtues of all
the herbs of the meadow. She can change her

form, and soar in the air like a bird; she can be where she pleases in a moment, and in a moment descend on our coasts from the clouds. Her sister Thiten is renowned for her skill on the harp.

"'With the prince we arrived, and Morgana received us with fitting honour. And in her own chamber she placed the king on a bed of gold, and with delicate touch, she uncovered the wound. Long she considered it, and at length said to him that she could heal it if he stayed long with her, and willed her to attempt her cure. Rejoiced at this news, we intrusted the king to her care, and soon after set sail.'"

Sir Thomas Malory, who wrote the book called the "Historie of King Arthur," or more commonly the "Morte d'Arthur," utters these high thoughts concerning the memory of the great king: —

"Oh, yee mightie and pompeous lords, shining in the glory transitory of this unstable life, as in raigning over great realmes and mightie great countries, fortified with strong castles and toures, edified with many a rich citie; yee also,

yee fierce and mightie knights, so valiant in
adventurous deeds of armes; behold, behold,
see how this mightie conquerour king Arthur,
whom in his humaine life all the world doubted,
see also the noble queene Guenever, which
sometime sat in her chaire adorned with gold,
pearles, and precious stones, now lye full low
in obscure fosse or pit, covered with clods of
earth and clay; behold also this mightie cham-
pion Sir Launcelot, pearelesse of all knighthood, see now how hee lyeth groveling upon
the cold mould, now being so feeble and faint
that sometime was so terrible. How and in
what manner ought yee to bee so desirous of
worldly honour so dangerous! Therefore mee
thinketh this present booke is right necessary
often to be read, for in it shall yee finde the
most gracious, knightly, and vertuous war of
the most noble knights of the world, whereby
they gat praysing continually. Also mee seem-
eth, by the oft reading thereof, yee shall greatly
desire to accustome your selfe in following of
those gracious knightly deedes, that is to say,
to dread God, and to love righteousnesse, faith-

fully and couragiously to serve your soveraigne prince; and the more that God hath given you the triumphall honour, the meeker yee ought to bee, ever feareing the unstablenesse of this deceitfull world."

# XI

## MAELDUIN'S VOYAGE

A N Irish knight named Maelduin set forth
early in the eighth century to seek
round the seas for his father's murderers. By the advice of a wizard, he was to
take with him seventeen companions, neither
less nor more; but at the last moment his three
foster brothers, whom he had not included,
begged to go with him. He refused, and they
cast themselves into the sea to swim after his
vessel. Maelduin had pity on them and took
them in, but his disregard of the wizard's advice
brought punishment; and it was only after long
wanderings, after visiting multitudes of unknown
and often enchanted islands, and after the death
or loss of the three foster brothers, that Maelduin
was able to return to his native land.

One island which they visited was divided
into four parts by four fences, one of gold, one

of silver, one of brass, one of crystal. In the
first division there dwelt kings, in the second
queens, in the third warriors, and in the fourth
maidens. The voyagers landed in the maidens'
realm; one of these came out in a boat and
gave them food, such that every one found in
it the taste he liked best; then followed an
enchanted drink, which made them sleep for
three days and three nights. When they
awakened they were in their boat on the sea,
and nothing was to be seen either of island or
maidens.

The next island had in it a fortress with a
brazen door and a bridge of glass, on which
every one who ascended it slipped and fell.
A woman came from the fortress, pail in hand,
drew water from the sea and returned, not
answering them when they spoke. When they
reached at last the brazen door and struck
upon it, it made a sweet and soothing sound,
and they went to sleep, for three days and
nights, as before. On the fourth day a
maiden came who was most beautiful; she wore
garments of white silk, a white mantle with a

H

brooch of silver with studs of gold, and a gold band round her hair. She greeted each man by his name, and said, "It is long that we have expected you." She took them into the castle and gave them every kind of food they had ever desired. Maelduin was filled with love for her and asked her for her love; but she told him that love was sin and she had no knowledge of sin; so she left him. On the morrow they found their boat, stranded on a crag, while lady and fortress and island had all vanished.

Another island on which they landed was large and bare, with another fortress and a palace. There they met a lady who was kinder. She wore an embroidered purple mantle, gold embroidered gloves, and ornamented sandals, and was just riding up to the palace door. Seventeen maidens waited there for her. She offered to keep the strangers as guests, and that each of them should have a wife, she herself wedding Maelduin. She was, it seems, the widow of the king of the island, and these were her seventeen daughters. She ruled the island and went every day to judge the people and direct

"The brazen door made a sweet and soothing sound, and they went to sleep for three days and nights. On the fourth day a maiden came who was most beautiful. She greeted each man and said, 'It is long that we have expected you.'" — p. 98

their lives. If the strangers would stay, she said that they should never more know sorrow, or hardships, or old age; she herself, in spite of her large family, being young and beautiful as ever. They stayed three months, and it seemed to all but Maelduin that the three months were three years. When the queen was absent, one day, the men took the boat and compelled Maelduin to leave the island with them; but the queen rode after them and flung a rope, which Maelduin caught and which clung to his hand. She drew them back to the shore; this happened thrice, and the men accused Maelduin of catching the rope on purpose; he bade another man catch it, and his companions cut off his hand, and they escaped at last.

On one island the seafarers found three magic apples, and each apple gave sufficient food for forty nights; again, on another island, they found the same apples. In another place still, a great bird like a cloud arrived, with a tree larger than an oak in its claws. After a while two eagles came and cleaned the feathers of the

larger bird. They also stripped off the red
berries from the tree and threw them into the
ocean until its foam grew red. The great
bird then flew into the ocean and cleaned itself.
This happened daily for three days, when the
great bird flew away with stronger wings, its
youth being thus renewed.

They came to another island where many
people stood by the shore talking and joking.
They were all looking at Maelduin and his comrades, and kept gaping and laughing, but would
not exchange a word with them. Then Maelduin sent one of his foster brothers on the island;
but he ranged himself with the others and did as
they did. Maelduin and his men rowed round
and round the island, and whenever they passed
the point where this comrade was, they addressed him, but he never answered, and only
gaped and laughed. They waited for him
a long time and left him. This island they
found to be called The Island of Joy.

On another island they found sheep grazing,
of enormous size; on another, birds, whose eggs
when eaten caused feathers to sprout all over the

bodies of those who eat them. On another they found crimson flowers, whose mere perfume sufficed for food, and they encountered women whose only food was apples. Through the window flew three birds : a blue one with a crimson head; a crimson one with a green head; a green one with a golden head. These sang heavenly music, and were sent to accompany the wanderers on their departing; the queen of the island gave them an emerald cup, such that water poured into it became wine. She asked if they knew how long they had been there, and when they said " a day," she told them that it was a year, during which they had had no food. As they sailed away, the birds sang to them until both birds and island disappeared in the mist.

They saw another island standing on a single pedestal, as if on one foot, projecting from the water. Rowing round it to seek a way into it they found no passage, but they saw in the base of the pedestal, under water, a closed door with a lock—this being the only way in which the island could be entered. Around another island there was a fiery rampart, which constantly moved in a circle. In the side of that rampart was an open door, and as it came opposite them in its turning course, they beheld through it the island and all therein; and its occupants, even human beings, were many and beautiful, wearing rich garments, and feasting with gold vessels in their hands. The voyagers lingered long to gaze upon this marvel.

On another island they found many human beings, black in color and raiment, and always bewailing. Lots were cast, and another of Maelduin's foster brothers was sent on shore. He at once joined the weeping crowd, and did as they did. Two others were sent to bring him back, and both shared his fate, falling under some strange spell. Then Maelduin sent four others, and bade them look neither at the land nor at the sky; to wrap their mouths and noses with their garments, and not breathe the island air; and not to take off their eyes from their comrades. In this way the two who followed the foster brother on shore were rescued, but he remained behind.

Of another island they could see nothing but

a fort, protected by a great white rampart, on which nothing living was to be seen but a small cat, leaping from one to another of four stone pillars. They found brooches and ornaments of gold and silver, they found white quilts and embroidered garments hanging up, flitches of bacon were suspended, a whole ox was roasting, and vessels stood filled with intoxicating drinks. Maelduin asked the cat if all this was for them; but the cat merely looked at him and went on playing. The seafarers dined and drank, then went to sleep. As they were about to depart, Maelduin's third foster brother proposed to carry off a tempting necklace, and in spite of his leader's warnings grasped it. Instantly the cat leaped through him like a fiery arrow, burned him so that he became ashes, and went back to its pillar. Thus all three of the foster brothers who had disregarded the wizard's warning, and forced themselves upon the party, were either killed or left behind upon the enchanted islands.

Around another island there was a demon horse-race going on; the riders were just riding in over the sea, and then the race began; the

voyagers could only dimly perceive the forms
of the horses, but could hear the cries of their
riders, the strokes of the whips, and the words
of the spectators, "See the gray horse!" "Watch
the chestnut horse!" and the voyagers were so
alarmed that they rowed away. The next
island was covered with trees laden with golden
apples, but these were being rapidly eaten by
small, scarlet animals which they found, on
coming nearer, to be all made of fire and thus
brightened in hue. Then the animals vanished,
and Maelduin with his men landed, and though
the ground was still hot from the fiery creatures,
they brought away a boat load of the apples.
Another island was divided into two parts by
a brass wall across the middle. There were
two flocks of sheep, and those on one side of
the wall were white, while the others were
black. A large man was dividing and arranging the sheep, and threw them easily over the
wall. When he threw a white sheep among
the black ones it became black, and when he
threw a black sheep among the white ones, it
became white instantly. The voyagers thought

of landing, but when Maelduin saw this, he said, "Let us throw something on shore to see if it will change color. If it does, we will avoid the island." So they took a black branch and threw it toward the white sheep. When it fell, it grew white; and the same with a white branch on the black side. "It is lucky for us," said Maelduin, "that we did not land on this island."

They came next to an island where there was but one man visible, very aged, and with long, white hair. Above him were trees, covered with great numbers of birds. The old man told them that he like them had come in a curragh, or coracle, and had placed many green sods beneath his feet, to steady the boat. Reaching this spot, the green sods had joined together and formed an island which at first gave him hardly room to stand; but every year one foot was added to its size, and one tree grew up. He had lived there for centuries, and those birds were the souls of his children and descendants, each of whom was sent there after death, and they were all fed from

heaven each day. On the next island there was
a great roaring as of bellows and a sound of
smiths' hammers, as if striking all together on
an anvil, every sound seeming to come from
the strokes of a dozen men. "Are they near?"
asked one big voice." "Silence!" said another;
and they were evidently watching for the boat.
When it rowed away, one of the smiths flung
after them a vast mass of red-hot iron, which he
had grasped with the tongs from the furnace.
It fell just short, but made the whole sea to
hiss and boil around them as they rowed away.

Another island had a wall of water round
it, and Maelduin and his men saw multitudes of
people driving away herds of cattle and sheep,
and shouting, "There they are, they have
come again;" and a woman pelted them from
below with great nuts, which the crew gathered
for eating. Then as they rowed away they
heard one man say, "Where are they now?"
and another cried, "They are going away."
Still again they visited an island where a great
stream of water shot up into the air and made
an arch like a rainbow that spanned the land.

They walked below it without getting wet, and hooked down from it many large salmon; besides that, many fell out above their heads, so that they had more than they could carry away with them. These are by no means all of the strange adventures of Maelduin and his men.

The last island to which they came was called Raven's Stream, and there one of the men, who had been very homesick, leaped out upon shore. As soon as he touched the land he became a heap of ashes, as if his body had lain in the earth a thousand years. This showed them for the first time during how vast a period they had been absent, and what a space they must have traversed. Instead of thirty enchanted islands they had visited thrice fifty, many of them twice or thrice as large as Ireland, whence the voyagers first came. In the wonderful experiences of their long lives they had apparently lost sight of the search which they had undertaken, for the murderers of Maelduin's father, since of them we hear no more. The island enchantment seems to have banished all other thoughts.

## XII

## THE VOYAGE OF ST. BRANDAN

THE young student Brandan was awakened in the morning by the crowing of the cock in the great Irish abbey where he dwelt; he rose, washed his face and hands and dressed himself, then passed into the chapel, where he prayed and sang until the dawn of the day. "With song comes courage" was the motto of the abbey. It was one of those institutions like great colonies, — church, library, farm, workshop, college, all in one, — of which Ireland in the sixth century was full, and which existed also elsewhere. Their extent is best seen by the modern traveller in the remains of the vast buildings at Tintern in England, scattered over a wide extent of country, where you keep coming upon walls and fragments of buildings which once formed a part of a single great institution, in which all the life

of the community was organized, as was the
case in the Spanish missions of California.  At
the abbey of Bangor in Wales, for instance,
there were two thousand four hundred men, —
all under the direction of a comparatively small
body of monks, who were trained to an amount
of organizing skill like that now needed for a
great railway system.  Some of these men were
occupied in various mechanic arts, some in min-
ing, but most of them in agriculture, which
they carried on with their own hands, without
the aid of animals, and in total silence.

Having thus labored in the fields until noon-
day, Brandan then returned that he might work
in the library, transcribing ancient manuscripts or
illustrating books of prayer.  Having to observe
silence, he wrote the name of the book to give to
the librarian, and if it were a Christian work, he
stretched out his hand, making motions with his
fingers as if turning over the leaves; but if it
were by a pagan author, the monk who asked for
it was required to scratch his ear as a dog does,
to show his contempt, because, the regulations
said, an unbeliever might well be compared to

that animal.[1]   Taking the book, he copied it
in the Scriptorium or library, or took it to his
cell, where he wrote all winter without a fire.
It is to such monks that we owe all our knowledge of the earliest history of England and
Ireland; though doubtless the hand that wrote
the histories of Gildas and Bede grew as tired
as that of Brandan, or as that of the monk who
wrote in the corner of a beautiful manuscript:
" He who does not know how to write imagines
it to be no labor; but though only three fingers
hold the pen, the whole body grows weary."
In the same way Brandan may have learned
music and have had an organ in his monastery,
or have had a school of art, painting beautiful
miniatures for the holy missals.  This was his
early life in the convent.

Once a day they were called to food; this
consisting for them of bread and vegetables
with no seasoning but salt, although better fare
was furnished for the sick and the aged, for

---

[1] *Adde ut aurem tangas digito sicut canis cum pede pruriens solet, quia nec
immerito infideles tali animanti comparantur.* — MARTÈNE, *De Antiq. Monach.
ritibus*, p. 289, qu. by Montalembert, Monks of the West (tr.) VI. 190.

travellers and the poor. These last numbered, at Easter time, some three or four hundred, who constantly came and went, and upon whom the monks and young disciples waited. After the meal the monks spent three hours in the chapel, on their knees, still silent; then they confessed in turn to the abbot and then sought their hard-earned rest. They held all things in common; no one even received a gift for himself. War never reached them; it was the rarest thing for an armed party to molest their composure; their domains were regarded as a haven for the stormy world. Because there were so many such places in Ireland, it was known as The Isle of Saints.

Brandan was sent after a time to other abbeys, where he could pursue especial studies, for they had six branches of learning,—grammar, rhetoric, dialectics, geometry, astronomy, and music. Thus he passed three years, and was then advised to go to an especial teacher in the mountains, who had particular modes of teaching certain branches. But this priest —he was an Italian—was suffering from pov-

erty, and could receive his guest but for a few
weeks. One day as Brandan sat studying, he
saw, the legend says, a white mouse come
from a crack in the wall, a visitor which climbed
upon his table and left there a grain of wheat.
Then the mouse paused, looked at the student,
then ran about the table, went away and reap-
peared with another grain, and another, up to
five. Brandan, who had at the very instant
learned his lesson, rose from his seat, followed
the mouse, and looking through a hole in the
wall, saw a great pile of wheat, stored in a concealed apartment. On his showing this to the
head of the convent, it was pronounced a miracle;
the food was distributed to the poor, and "the
people blessed his charity while the Lord blessed
his studies."

In the course of years, Brandan became himself the head of one of the great abbeys, that of
Clonfert, of the order of St. Benedict, where he
had under him nearly three thousand monks.
In this abbey, having one day given hospitality
to a monk named Berinthus, who had just returned from an ocean voyage, Brandan learned

from him the existence, far off in the ocean, of
an island called The Delicious Isle, to which a
priest named Mernoc had retired, with many
companions of his order.   Berinthus found Mernoc and the other monks living apart from one
another for purposes of prayer, but when they
came together, Mernoc said, they were like bees
from different beehives.   They met for their
food and for church ;  their food included only
apples, nuts, and various herbs.   One day Mernoc said to Berinthus, " I will conduct you to the
Promised Isle of the Saints."   So they went on
board a little ship and sailed westward through
a thick fog until a great light shone and they
found themselves near an island which was large
and fruitful and bore many apples.   There were
no herbs without blossoms, he said, nor trees
without fruits, and there were precious stones,
and the island was traversed by a great river.
Then they met a man of shining aspect who told
them that they had without knowing it passed
a year already in the island ;  that they had
needed neither food nor sleep.   Then they returned to the Delicious Island, and every one

I

knew where they had been by the perfume of their garments. This was the story of Berinthus, and from this time forward nothing could keep Brandan from the purpose of beholding for himself these blessed islands.

Before carrying out his plans, however, he went, about the year 560, to visit an abbot named Enda, who lived at Arran, then called Isle of the Saints, a priest who was supposed to know more than any one concerning the farther lands of the western sea. He knew, for instance, of the enchanted island named Hy-Brasail, which could be seen from the coast of Ireland only once in seven years, and which the priests had vainly tried to disenchant. Some islands, it was believed, had been already disenchanted by throwing on them a few sparks of lighted turf; but as Hy-Brasail was too far for this, there were repeated efforts to disenchant it by shooting fiery arrows towards it, though this had not yet been successful. Then Enda could tell of wonderful ways to cross the sea without a boat, how his sister Fanchea had done it by spreading her own cloak upon the waves,

and how she and three other nuns were borne
upon it.  She found, however, that one hem of
the cloak sank below the water, because one of
her companions had brought with her, against
orders, a brazen vessel from the convent; but
on her throwing it away, the sinking hem rose to
the level of the rest and bore them safely.  St.
Enda himself had first crossed to Arran on a
large stone which he had ordered his followers
to place on the water and which floated before
the wind; and he told of another priest who had
walked on the sea as on a meadow and plucked
flowers as he went.  Hearing such tales, how
could St. Brandan fear to enter on his voyage?

He caused a boat to be built of a fashion
which one may still see in Welsh and Irish
rivers, and known as a curragh or coracle;
made of an osier frame covered with tanned and
oiled skins.  He took with him seventeen priests,
among whom was St. Malo, then a mere boy,
but afterwards celebrated.  They sailed to the
southwest, and after being forty days at sea they
reached a rocky island furrowed with streams,
where they received the kindest hospitality, and

took in fresh provisions. They sailed again the next day, and found themselves entangled in contrary currents and perplexing winds, so that they were long in reaching another island, green and fertile, watered by rivers which were full of fish, and covered with vast herds of sheep as large as heifers. Here they renewed their stock of provisions, and chose a spotless lamb with which to celebrate Easter Sunday on another island, which they saw at a short distance.

This island was wholly bare, without sandy shores or wooded slopes, and they all landed upon it to cook their lamb; but when they had arranged their cooking-apparatus, and when their fire began to blaze, the island seemed to move beneath their feet, and they ran in terror to their boat, from which Brandan had not yet landed. Their supposed island was a whale, and they rowed hastily away from it toward the island they had left, while the whale glided away, still showing, at a distance of two miles, the fire blazing on his back.

The next island they visited was wooded and fertile, where they found a multitude of birds, which chanted with them the praises of the Lord, so that they called this the Paradise of Birds.

This was the description given of this island by an old writer named Wynkyn de Worde, in "The Golden Legend": —

"Soon after, as God would, they saw a fair island, full of flowers, herbs, and trees, whereof they thanked God of his good grace; and anon they went on land, and when they had gone long in this, they found a full fayre well, and thereby stood a fair tree full of boughs, and on every bough sat a fayre bird, and they sat so thick on the tree that uneath [scarcely] any leaf of the tree might be seen. The number of them was so great, and they sang so merrilie, that it was an heavenlie noise to hear. Whereupon St. Brandan kneeled down on his knees and wept for joy, and made his praise devoutlie to our Lord God, to know what these birds meant. And then anon one of the birds flew from the tree to St. Brandan, and he with the flickering of his wings made a full merrie noise like a fiddle, that him seemed he never heard so joyful a melodie. And then St. Brandan commanded the foule to tell him the cause why they sat so thick on the tree and sang so merrilie. And then the foule said, some time we were angels in heaven, but when our master, Lucifer, fell down into hell for his high pride, and we fell with him for our offences, some higher and some lower, after the quality of the trespasse. And because our trespasse is so little, therefore our Lord hath sent us here, out of all paine, in full great joy and mirthe, after his pleasing, here to serve him on this tree in the best manner we can. The Sundaie is a daie of rest from all worldly occupation, and therefore that day all we be made as white as any snow, for to praise our Lorde in the best wise we may. And then all the birds began to sing evensong so merrilie that it was an heavenlie noise to hear; and after supper St. Brandan and his fellows went to bed and slept well. And in the morn they arose by times, and then those foules began mattyns, prime, and hours, and all such service as Christian men used to sing; and St. Brandan, with his fellows, abode there seven weeks, until Trinity Sunday was passed."

Having then embarked, they wandered for
months on the ocean, before reaching another
island.  That on which they finally landed was
inhabited by monks who had as their patrons
St. Patrick and St. Ailbée, and they spent
Christmas there.  A year passed in these voyages, and the tradition is that for six other
years they made just the same circuit, always
spending Holy Week at the island where they
found the sheep, alighting for Easter on the
back of the same patient whale, visiting the
Isle of Birds at Pentecost, and reaching
the island of St. Patrick and St. Ailbée in
time for Christmas.

But in the seventh year they met with
wholly new perils.  They were attacked, the
legend says, first by a whale, then by a griffin,
and then by a race of cyclops, or one-eyed
giants.  Then they came to an island where
the whale which had attacked them was thrown
on shore, so that they could cut him to pieces;
then another island which had great fruits, and
was called The Island of the Strong Man; and
lastly one where the grapes filled the air with

perfume. After this they saw an island, all cinders and flames, where the cyclops had their forges, and they sailed away in the light of an immense fire. The next day they saw, looking northward, a great and high mountain sending out flames at the top. Turning hastily. from this dreadful sight, they saw a little round island, at the top of which a hermit dwelt, who gave them his benediction. Then they sailed southward once more, and stopped at their usual places of resort for Holy Week, Easter, and Whitsuntide.

It was on this trip that they had, so the legend says, that strange interview with Judas Iscariot, out of which Matthew Arnold has made a ballad. Sailing in the wintry northern seas at Christmas time, St. Brandan saw an iceberg floating by, on which a human form rested motionless; and when it moved at last, he saw by its resemblance to the painted pictures he had seen that it must be Judas Iscariot, who had died five centuries before. Then as the boat floated near the iceberg, Judas spoke and told him his tale. After he had betrayed Jesus Christ, after he had died, and had been consigned to the flames of hell, — which were believed in very literally in those days, — an angel came to him on Christmas night and said that he might go thence and cool himself for an hour. " Why this mercy ? " asked Judas Iscariot. Then the angel said to him, " Remember the leper in Joppa," and poor Judas recalled how once when the hot wind, called the sirocco, swept through the streets of Joppa, and he saw a naked leper by the wayside, sitting in agony from the heat and the drifting sand, Judas had thrown his cloak over him for a shelter and received his thanks. In reward for this, the angel now told him, he was to have, once a year, an hour's respite from his pain ; he was allowed in that hour to fling himself on an iceberg and cool his burning heat as he drifted through the northern seas. Then St. Brandan bent his head in prayer ; and when he looked up, the hour was passed, and Judas had been hurried back into his torments.

It seems to have been only after seven years

of this wandering that they at last penetrated within the obscure fogs which surrounded the Isle of the Saints, and came upon a shore which lay all bathed in sunny light. It was a vast island, sprinkled with precious stones, and covered with ripe fruits; they traversed it for forty days without arriving at the end, though they reached a great river which flowed through the midst of it from east to west. There an angel appeared to them, and told them that they could go no farther, but could return to their own abode, carrying from the island some of those fruits and precious stones which were reserved to be distributed among the saints when all the world should be brought to the true faith. In order to hasten that time, it appears that St. Malo, the youngest of the sea-faring monks, had wished, in his zeal, to baptize some one, and had there-fore dug up a heathen giant who had been, for some reason, buried on the blessed isle. Not only had he dug the giant's body up, but St. Malo had brought him to life again sufficiently for the purpose of baptism and instruction in the true faith; after which he gave him the name

of Mildus, and let him die once more and be
reburied.   Then, facing homeward and sailing
beyond the fog, they touched once more at The
Island of Delights, received the benediction of
the abbot of the monastery, and sailed for Ireland to tell their brethren of the wonders they
had seen.

He used to tell them especially to his nurse
Ita, under whose care he had been placed until
his fifth year.   His monastery at Clonfert grew,
as has been said, to include three thousand
monks; and he spent his remaining years in
peace and sanctity.   The supposed islands
which he visited are still believed by many to
have formed a part of the American continent,
and he is still thought by some Irish scholars to
have been the first to discover this hemisphere,
nearly a thousand years before Columbus,
although this view has not yet made much impression on historians.   The Paradise of Birds,
in particular, has been placed by these scholars
in Mexico, and an Irish poet has written a long
poem describing the delights to be found
there : —

" Oft, in the sunny mornings, have I seen
　　Bright yellow birds, of a rich lemon hue,
Meeting in crowds upon the branches green,
　　And sweetly singing all the morning through;
And others, with their heads grayish and dark,
　　Pressing their cinnamon cheeks to the old trees,
And striking on the hard, rough, shrivelled bark,
　　Like conscience on a bosom ill at ease.

" And diamond-birds chirping their single notes,
　　Now 'mid the trumpet-flower's deep blossoms seen,
Now floating brightly on with fiery throats —
　　Small winged emeralds of golden green;
And other larger birds with orange cheeks,
　　A many-color-painted, chattering crowd,
Prattling forever with their curved beaks,
　　And through the silent woods screaming aloud."

# XIII

## KIRWAN'S SEARCH FOR HY–BRASAIL

THE boy Kirwan lay on one of the steep cliffs of the Island of Innismane — one of the islands of Arran, formerly called Isles of the Saints. He was looking across the Atlantic for a glimpse of Hy-Brasail. This was what they called it; it was a mysterious island which Kirwan's grandfather had seen, or thought he had seen — and Kirwan's father also; — indeed, there was not one of the old people on the island who did not think he had seen it, and the older they were, the oftener it had been seen by them, and the larger it looked. But Kirwan had never seen it, and whenever he came to the top of the highest cliff, where he often went bird-nesting, he climbed the great mass of granite called The Gregory, and peered out into the west, especially at sunset, in hopes that he would at least catch a glimpse, some happy evening, of the cliffs and meadows of Hy-Brasail. But as yet he had never espied them. All this was more than two hundred years ago.

He naturally went up to The Gregory at this hour, because it was then that he met the other boys, and caught puffins by being lowered over the cliff. The agent of the island employed the boys, and paid them a sixpence for every dozen birds, that he might sell the feathers. The boys had a rope three hundred feet long, which could reach the bottom of the cliff. One of them tied this rope around his waist, and then held it fast with both hands, the rope being held above by four or five strong boys, who lowered the cragman, or "clifter," as he was called, over the precipice. Kirwan was thus lowered to the rocks near the sea, where the puffins bred; and, loosening the rope, he prepared to spend the night in catching them. He had a pole with a snare on the end, which he easily clapped on the heads of the heavy and stupid birds; then tied each on a string as he caught it, and so kept it to be hauled up

in the morning.  He took in this way twenty
or thirty score of the birds, besides quantities
of their large eggs, which were found in deep
clefts in the rock; and these he carried with
him when his friends came in the morning to
haul him up.  It was a good school of courage, for sometimes boys missed their footing
and were dashed to pieces.  At other times he
fished in his father's boat, or drove calves for
sale on the mainland, or cured salt after high
tide in the caverns, or collected kelp for the
farmers.  But he was always looking forward
to a time when he might get a glimpse of the
island of Hy-Brasail, and make his way to it.

One day when all the fleet of fishing-boats
was out for the herring fishery, and Kirwan
among them, the fog came in closer and closer,
and he was shut apart from all others.  His
companion in the boat — or dory-mate, as it
would be called in New England — had gone
to cut bait on board another boat, but Kirwan
could manage the boat well enough alone.
Long he toiled with his oars toward the west,
where he fancied the rest of the fleet to be; and

sometimes he spread his little sprit-sail, steer-
ing with an oar — a thing which was, in a heavy
sea, almost as hard as rowing. At last the
fog lifted, and he found himself alone upon the
ocean. He had lost his bearings and could not
tell the points of the compass. Presently out
of a heavy bank of fog which rose against the
horizon he saw what seemed land. It gave
him new strength, and he worked hard to reach
it; but it was long since he had eaten, his head
was dizzy, and he lay down on the thwart of
the boat, rather heedless of what might come.
Growing weaker and weaker, he did not clearly
know what he was doing. Suddenly he started
up, for a voice hailed him from above his head.
He saw above him the high stern of a small
vessel, and with the aid of a sailor he was helped
on board.

He found himself on the deck of a sloop of
about seventy tons, John Nisbet, master, with a
crew of seven men. They had sailed from Kille-
begs (County Donegal), in Ireland, for the coast
of France, laden with butter, tallow, and hides,
and were now returning from France with French

wines, and were befogged as Kirwan had been.
The boy was at once taken on board and rated
as a seaman; and the later adventures of the
trip are here given as he reported them on his
return with the ship some months later.

The mist continued thicker and thicker for a
time, and when it suddenly furled itself away,
they found themselves on an unknown coast, with
the wind driving them shoreward.   There were
men on board who were familiar with the whole
coast of Ireland and Scotland, but they remembered nothing like this.   Finding less than three
fathoms of water, they came to anchor and sent
four men ashore to find where they were; these
being James Ross the carpenter and two sailors,
with the boy Kirwan.   They took swords and
pistols.   Landing at the edge of a little wood,
they walked for a mile within a pleasant valley
where cattle, horses, and sheep were feeding, and
then came in sight of a castle, small but strong,
where they went to the door and knocked.   No
one answered, and they walked on, up a green
hill, where there were multitudes of black rabbits; but when they had reached the top and

K

looked around they could see no inhabitants, nor any house; on which they returned to the sloop and told their tale. After this the whole ship's company went ashore, except one left in charge, and they wandered about for hours, yet saw nothing more. As night came on they made a fire at the base of a fallen oak, near the shore, and lay around it, talking, and smoking the lately discovered weed, tobacco; when suddenly they heard loud noises from the direction of the castle and then all over the island, which frightened them so that they went on board the sloop and stayed all night.

The next morning they saw a dignified, elderly gentleman with ten unarmed followers coming down towards the shore. Hailing the sloop, the older gentleman, speaking Gaelic, asked who and whence they were, and being told, invited them ashore as his guests. They went on shore, well armed; and he embraced them one by one, telling them that they were the happiest sight that island had seen for hundreds of years; that it was called Hy-Brasail or O-Brazile; that his ancestors had been princes

of it, but for many years it had been taken possession of by enchanters, who kept it almost
always invisible, so that no ship came there;
and that for the same reason he and his friends
were rendered unable to answer the sailors, even
when they knocked at the door; and that the
enchantment must remain until a fire was kindled on the island by good Christians. This
had been done the night before, and the terrible
noises which they had heard were from the
powers of darkness, which had now left the
island forever.

And indeed when the sailors were led to the
castle, they saw that the chief tower had just
been demolished by the powers of darkness,
as they retreated; but there were sitting within
the halls men and women of dignified appearance,
who thanked them for the good service they
had done. Then they were taken over the
island, which proved to be some sixty miles
long and thirty wide, abounding with horses,
cattle, sheep, deer, rabbits, and birds, but without
any swine; it had also rich mines of silver and
gold, but few people, although there were ruins

of old towns and cities. The sailors, after being richly rewarded, were sent on board their vessel and furnished with sailing directions to their port. On reaching home, they showed to the minister of their town the pieces of gold and silver that were given them at the island, these being of an ancient stamp, somewhat rusty yet of pure gold; and there was at once an eager desire on the part of certain of the townsmen to go with them. Within a week an expedition was fitted out, containing several godly ministers, who wished to visit and discover the inhabitants of the island; but through some mishap of the seas this expedition was never heard of again.

Partly for this reason and partly because none of Captain Nesbit's crew wished to return to the island, there came to be in time a feeling of distrust about all this rediscovery of Hy-Brasail or O-Brazile. There were not wanting those who held that the ancient gold pieces might have been gained by piracy, such as was beginning to be known upon the Spanish main; and as for the boy Kirwan, some of his playmates did not hesitate to express the opinion that he had always been, as they phrased it, the greatest liar that ever spoke. What is certain is that the island of Brazil or Hy-Brasail had appeared on maps ever since 1367 as being near the coast of Ireland; that many voyages were made from Bristol to find it, a hundred years later; that it was mentioned about 1636 as often seen from the shore; and that it appeared as Brazil Rock on the London Admiralty Charts until after 1850. If many people tried to find it and failed, why should not Kirwan have tried and succeeded? And as to his stretching his story a little by throwing in a few enchanters and magic castles, there was not a voyager of his period who was not tempted to do the same.

# XIV

## THE ISLE OF SATAN'S HAND

THE prosperous farmer Conall Ua Corra
in the province of Connaught had everything to make him happy except that he
and his wife had no children to cheer their old
age and inherit their estate. Conall had prayed
for children, and one day said in his impatience
that he would rather have them sent by Satan
than not have them at all. A year or two later
his wife had three sons at a birth, and when
these sons came to maturity, they were so
ridiculed by other young men, as being the
sons of Satan, that they said, " If such is really
our parentage, we will do Satan's work." So
they collected around them a few villains and
began plundering and destroying the churches
in the neighborhood and thus injuring half the
church buildings in the country. At last they
resolved to visit also the church of Clothar, to

destroy it, and to kill if necessary their mother's father, who was the leading layman of the parish. When they came to the church, they found the old man on the green in front of it, distributing meat and drink to his tenants and the people of the parish. Seeing this, they postponed their plans until after dark and in the meantime went home with their grandfather, to spend the night at his house. They went to rest, and the eldest, Lochan, had a terrible dream in which he saw first the joys of heaven and then the terrors of future punishment, and then he awoke in dismay. Waking his brothers, he told them his dream, and that he now saw that they had been serving evil masters and making war upon a good one. Such was his bitterness of remorse that he converted them to his views, and they agreed to go to their grandfather in the morning, renounce their sinful ways and ask his pardon.

This they did, and he advised them to go to a celebrated saint, Finnen of Clonard, and take him as their spiritual guide. Laying aside their armor and weapons, they went to Clonard, where all the people, dreading them and knowing their wickedness, fled for their lives, except the saint himself, who came forward to meet them. With him the three brothers undertook the most austere religious exercises, and after a year they came to St. Finnen and asked his punishment for their former crimes. " You cannot," he said, " restore to life those you have slain, but you can at least restore the buildings you have devastated and ruined." So they went and repaired many churches, after which they resolved to go on a pilgrimage upon the great Atlantic Ocean. They built for themselves therefore a curragh or coracle, covered with hides three deep. It was capable of carrying nine persons, and they selected five out of the many who wished to join the party. There were a bishop, a priest, a deacon, a musician, and the man who had modelled the boat; and with these they pushed out to sea.

It had happened some years before that in a quarrel about a deer hunt, the men of Ross had killed the king. It had been decided that, by way of punishment, sixty couples of the people of Ross should be sent out to sea, two

and two, in small boats, to meet what fate they
might upon the deeps. They were watched
that they might not land again, and for many
years nothing more had been heard from them.
The most pious task which these repenting
pilgrims could undertake, it was thought, would
be to seek these banished people. They resolved to spread their sail and let Providence
direct their course. They went, therefore, northwest on the Atlantic, where they visited several
wonderful islands, on one of which there was a
great bird which related to them, the legend
says, the whole history of the world, and gave
them a great leaf from a tree — the leaf being
as large as an ox-hide, and being preserved for
many years in one of the churches after their
return. At the next island they heard sweet
human voices, and found that the sixty banished couples had established their homes there.

The pilgrims then went onward in their hide-
bound boat until they reached the coast of
Spain, and there they landed and dwelt for a
time. The bishop built a church, and the
priest officiated in it, and the organist took

charge of the music. All prospered; yet the boat-builder and the three brothers were never quite contented, for they had roamed the seas too long; and they longed for a new enterprise for their idle valor. They thought they had found this when one day they found on the sea-coast a group of women tearing their hair, and when they asked the explanation, "Señor," said an old woman, "our sons and our husbands have again fallen into the hand of Satan." At this the three brothers were startled, for they remembered well how they used, in youth, to rank themselves as Satan's children. Asking farther, they learned that a shattered boat they saw on the beach was one of a pair of boats which had been carried too far out to sea, and had come near an islet which the sailors called *Isla de la Man Satanaxio*, or The Island of Satan's Hand. It appeared that in that region there was an islet so called, always surrounded by chilly mists and water of a deadly cold; that no one had ever reached it, as it constantly changed place; but that a demon hand sometimes uprose from it,

" A demon hand sometimes uprose from the islet and plucked away men and even
whole boats, which, when once grasped, usually by night, were never seen again,
but perished helplessly.'' — p. 139

and plucked away men and even whole boats, which, when once grasped, usually by night, were never seen again, but perished helplessly, victims of Satan's Hand.

When the voyagers laughed at this legend, the priest of the village showed them, on the early chart of Bianco, the name of " De la Man Satanagio," and on that of Beccaria the name " Satanagio" alone, both these being the titles of islands. Not alarmed at the name of Satan, as being that of one whom they had supposed, in their days of darkness, to be their patron, they pushed boldly out to sea and steered westward, a boat-load of Spanish fishermen following in their wake. Passing island after island of green and fertile look, they found themselves at last in what seemed a less favored zone — as windy as the " roaring forties," and growing chillier every hour. Fogs gathered quickly, so that they could scarcely see the companion boat, and the Spanish fishermen called out to them, " Garda da la Man do Satanaxio!" (" Look out for Satan's hand!")

As they cried, the fog became denser yet,

and when it once parted for a moment, something that lifted itself high above them, like a
gigantic hand, showed itself an instant, and
then descended with a crushing grasp upon
the boat of the Spanish fishermen, breaking it
to pieces, and dragging some of the men below the water, while others, escaping, swam
through the ice-cold waves, and were with
difficulty taken on board the coracle; this
being all the harder because the whole surface
of the water was boiling and seething furiously.
Rowing away as they could from this perilous
neighborhood, they lay on their oars when the
night came on, not knowing which way to go.
Gradually the fog cleared away, the sun rose
clearly at last, and wherever they looked on
the deep they saw no traces of any island, still
less of the demon hand. But for the presence
among them of the fishermen they had picked
up, there was nothing to show that any casualty
had happened.

That day they steered still farther to the
west with some repining from the crew, and at
night the same fog gathered, the same deadly

chill came on. Finding themselves in shoal
water, and apparently near some island, they
decided to anchor the boat; and as the man
in the bow bent over to clear away the anchor,
something came down upon him with the same
awful force, and knocked him overboard. His
body could not be recovered, and as the wind
came up, they drove before it until noon of the
next day, seeing nothing of any land and the
ocean deepening again. By noon the fog
cleared, and they saw nothing, but cried with
one voice that the boat should be put about,
and they should return to Spain. For two
days they rowed in peace over a summer sea;
then came the fog again and they laid on their
oars that night. All around them dim islands
seemed to float, scarcely discernible in the fog;
sometimes from the top of each a point would
show itself, as of a mighty hand, and they
could hear an occasional plash and roar, as if
this hand came downwards. Once they heard
a cry, as if of sailors from another vessel.
Then they strained their eyes to gaze into the
fog, and a whole island seemed to be turning

itself upside down, its peak coming down, while its base went uppermost, and the whole water boiled for leagues around, as if both earth and sea were upheaved.

The sun rose upon this chaos of waters. No demon hand was anywhere visible, nor any island, but a few icebergs were in sight, and the frightened sailors rowed away and made sail for home. It was rare to see icebergs so far south, and this naturally added to the general dismay. Amid the superstition of the sailors, the tales grew and grew, and all the terrors became mingled. But tradition says that there were some veteran Spanish sailors along that coast, men who had sailed on longer voyages, and that these persons actually laughed at the whole story of Satan's Hand, saying that any one who had happened to see an iceberg topple over would know all about it. It was more generally believed, however, that all this was mere envy and jealousy; the daring fishermen remained heroes for the rest of their days; and it was only within a century or two that the island of Satanaxio disappeared from the charts.

# XV

## ANTILLIA, THE ISLAND OF THE SEVEN CITIES

THE young Spanish page, Luis de Vega, had been for some months at the court of Don Rodrigo, king of Spain, when he heard the old knights lamenting, as they came out of the palace at Toledo, over the king's last and most daring whim. "He means," said one of them in a whisper, "to penetrate the secret cave of the Gothic kings, that cave on which each successive sovereign has put a padlock."

"Till there are now twenty-seven of them," interrupted a still older knight.

"And he means," said the first, frowning at the interruption, "to take thence the treasures of his ancestors."

"Indeed, he must do it," said another, "else the son of his ancestors will have no treasure left of his own."

"But there is a spell upon it," said the other.

"For ages Spain has been threatened with invasion, and it is the old tradition that the only talisman which can prevent it is in this cave."

"Well," said the scoffer, "it is only by entering the cave that he can possess the talisman."

"But if he penetrates to it, his power is lost."

"A pretty talisman," said the other. "It is only of use to anybody so long as no one sees it. Were I the king I would hold it in my hands. And I have counselled him to heed no graybeards, but to seize the treasure for himself. I have offered to accompany him."

"May it please your lordship," said the eager Luis, "may I go with you?"

"Yes," said Don Alonzo de Carregas, turning to the ardent boy. "Where the king goes I go, and where I go thou shalt be my companion. See, señors," he said, turning to the others, "how the ready faith of boyhood puts your fears to shame. To his Majesty the terrors of this goblin cave are but a jest which frightens the old and only rouses the young to courage. The king may find the recesses of the cavern filled with gold and jewels; he

who goes with him may share them.   This boy
is my first recruit: who follows?"

By this time a whole group of courtiers, young
and old, had assembled about Don Alonzo, and
every man below thirty years was ready to
pledge himself to the enterprise.   But the older
courtiers and the archbishop Oppas were beseeching the king to refrain.   "Respect, O
king," they said, "the custom held sacred by
twenty-seven of thy predecessors.   Give us but
an estimate of the sum that may, in thy kingly
mind, represent the wealth that is within the
cavern walls, and we will raise it on our own
domains, rather than see the sacred tradition
set at nought."   The king's only answer was,
"Follow me," Don Alonzo hastily sending the
boy Luis to collect the younger knights who
had already pledged themselves to the enterprise.   A gallant troop, they made their way
down the steep steps which led from the palace
to the cave.   The news had spread; the ladies
had gathered on the balconies, and the bright
face of one laughing girl looked from a bower
window, while she tossed a rose to the happy

L

Luis. Alas, it fell short of its mark and hit the robes of Archbishop Oppas, who stood with frowning face as the youngster swept by. The archbishop crushed it unwittingly in the hand that held the crosier.

The rusty padlocks were broken, and each fell clanking on the floor, and was brushed away by mailed heels. They passed from room to room with torches, for the cavern extended far beneath the earth; yet they found no treasure save the jewelled table of Solomon. But for their great expectations, this table alone might have proved sufficient to reward their act of daring. Some believed that it had been brought by the Romans from Solomon's temple, and from Rome by the Goths and Vandals who sacked that city and afterwards conquered Spain; but all believed it to be sacred, and now saw it to be gorgeous. Some describe it as being of gold, set with precious stones; others, as of gold and silver, making it yellow and white in hue, ornamented with a row of pearls, a row of rubies, and another row of emeralds. It is generally agreed that it stood on three hundred and

sixty feet, each made of a single emerald.  Being
what it was, the king did not venture to remove
it, but left it where it was.  Traversing chamber
after chamber and finding all empty, they at
last found all passages leading to the inmost
apartment, which had a marble urn in the centre.
Yet all eyes presently turned from this urn to
a large painting on the wall which displayed a
troop of horsemen in full motion.  Their
horses were of Arab breed, their arms were
scimitars and lances, with fluttering pennons;
they wore turbans, and their coarse black hair
fell over their shoulders; they were dressed in
skins.  Never had there been seen by the courtiers a mounted troop so wild, so eager, so formidable.  Turning from them to the marble
urn, the king drew from it a parchment, which
said: "These are the people who, whenever this
cave is entered and the spell contained in this
urn is broken, shall possess this country.  An
idle curiosity has done its work." [1]

[1] " *Latinas letras á la margen puestas*
*Decian : — ' Cuando aquesta puerta y arca*
*Fueran abiertas, gentes como estas*
*Pondrán por tierra cuanto España abarca.' "*
—LOPE DE VEGA.

The rash king, covering his eyes with his hands, fled outward from the cavern; his knights followed him, but Don Alonzo lingered last except the boy Luis. "Nevertheless, my lord," said Luis, "I should like to strike a blow at these bold barbarians." "We may have an opportunity," said the gloomy knight. He closed the centre gate of the cavern, and tried to replace the broken padlocks, but it was in vain. In twenty-four hours the story had travelled over the kingdom.

The boy Luis little knew into what a complex plot he was drifting. In the secret soul of his protector, Don Alonzo, there burned a great anger against the weak and licentious king. He and his father, Count Julian, and Archbishop Oppas, his uncle, were secretly brooding plans of wrath against Don Rodrigo for his ill treatment of Don Alonzo's sister, Florinda. Rumors had told them that an army of strange warriors from Africa, who had hitherto carried all before them, were threatening to cross the straits not yet called Gibraltar, and descend on Spain. All the ties of fidelity held these courtiers to the king; but they secretly hated him, and wished for his downfall. By the next day they had planned to betray him to the Moors. Count Julian had come to make his military report to Don Rodrigo, and on some pretext had withdrawn Florinda from the court. "When you come again," said the pleasure-loving king, "bring me some hawks from the south, that we may again go hawking." "I will bring you hawks enough," was the answer, "and such as you never saw before." "But Rodrigo," says the Arabian chronicler, "did not understand the full meaning of his words."

It was a hard blow for the young Luis when he discovered what a plot was being urged around him. He would gladly have been faithful to the king, worthless as he knew him to be; but Don Alonzo had been his benefactor, and he held by him. Meanwhile the conspiracy drew towards completion, and the Arab force was drawing nearer to the straits. A single foray into Spain had shown Musa, the Arab general, the weakness of the kingdom; that the cities were unfortified, the citizens unarmed, and many of the nobles lukewarm towards the king. "Hasten," he said, "towards that country where the palaces are filled with gold and silver, and the men cannot fight in their defence." Accordingly, in the early spring of the year 711, Musa sent his next in command, Tarik, to cross to Spain with an army of seven thousand men, consisting mostly of chosen cavalry. They crossed the straits then called the Sea of Narrowness, embarking the troops at Tangier and Ceute in many merchant vessels, and landing at that famous promontory called thenceforth by the Arab general's name, the Rock of Tarik, Dschebel-Tarik, or, more briefly, Gibraltar.

Luis, under Don Alonzo, was with the Spanish troops sent hastily down to resist the Arab invaders, and, as these troops were mounted, he had many opportunities of seeing the new enemies and observing their ways. They were a picturesque horde; their breasts were covered with mail armor; they wore white turbans on their heads, carried their bows slung across their backs, and their swords suspended to their girdles, while they held their long spears firmly grasped in their hands. The Arabs said that their fashion of mail armor had come to them from King David, "to whom," they said, "God made iron soft, and it became in his hands as thread." More than half of them were mounted on the swift horses which were peculiar to their people; and the white, red, and black turbans and cloaks made a most striking picture around the camp-fires. These men, too, were already trained and successful soldiers, held together both by a common religion and by the hope of spoil. There were twelve thousand of them by the most probable estimate, — for Musa had sent reinforcements, — and they had against them from five to eight times their number. But of the Spaniards only a small part were armed or drilled, or used to warfare, and great multitudes of them had to put their reliance in clubs, slings, axes, and short scythes. The cavalry were on the wings, where Luis found himself, with Count Julian and Archbishop Oppas to command them. Soon, however, Don Alonzo and Luis were detached, with others, to act as escort to the king, Don Rodrigo.

The battle began soon after daybreak on Sunday, July 19, 711. As the Spanish troops advanced, their trumpets sounded defiance and were answered by Moorish horns and kettle-drums. While they drew near, the shouts of the Spaniards were drowned in the *lelie* of the Arabs, the phrase *Lá ilá-ha ella-llah* — there is no deity but God. As they came nearer yet, there is a tradition that Rodrigo looking on the Moslem, said, " By the faith of the Messiah, these are the very men I saw painted on the walls of the cave at Toledo." Yet he certainly bore himself like a king, and he rode on the battle-field in a chariot of ivory lined with gold, having a silken awning decked with pearls and rubies, while the vehicle was drawn by three white mules abreast. He was then nearly eighty, and was dressed in a silken robe embroidered with pearls. He had brought with him in carts and on mules his treasures in jewels and money; and he had trains of mules whose only load consisted of ropes, to bind the arms of his captives, so sure was he of making every Arab his prisoner. Driving along the lines he addressed his troops boldly, and arriving at the centre quitted his chariot, put on a horned helmet, and mounted his white horse Orelio.

This was before the invention of gunpowder, and all battles were hand to hand. On the first day the result was doubtful, and Tarik rode through the Arab ranks, calling on them to fight for their religion and their safety. As the onset began, Tarik rode furiously at a Spanish chief whom he took for the king, and struck him down. For a moment it was believed to be the king whom he had killed, and from that moment new energy was given to the Arabs. The line of the Spaniards wavered; and at this moment the whole wing of cavalry to which Luis belonged rode out from its place and passed on the flank of the army, avoiding both Spaniard and Arab. "What means this?" said Luis to the horseman by his side. "It means," was the answer, "that Bishop Oppas is betraying the king." At this moment Don Alonzo rode up and cheered their march with explanations. "No more," he said, "will we obey this imbecile old king who can neither fight nor govern. He and his troops are but so many old women; it is only these Arabs who are men. All is arranged with Tarik, and we will save our country by joining the only man who can govern it." Luis groaned in dismay; it seemed to him an act of despicable treachery; but those around him seemed mostly prepared for it, and he said to himself, "After all, Don Alonzo is my chief; I must hold by him;" so he kept with the others, and the whole cavalry wing followed Oppas to a knoll, whence they watched the fight. It soon became a panic; the Arabs carried all before them, and the king himself was either killed or hid himself in a convent.

Many a Spaniard of the seceding wing of cavalry reproached himself afterwards for what had been done; and while the archbishop had some influence with the conquering general and persuaded him to allow the Christians everywhere to retain a part of their churches, yet he had, after all, the reward of a traitor in contempt and self-reproach. This he could bear no longer, and organizing an expedition from a Spanish port, he and six minor bishops, with many families of the Christians, made their way towards Gibraltar. They did not make their escape, however, without attracting notice and obstruction. As they rode among the hills with their long train, soldiers, ecclesiastics, women, and children, they saw a galloping band of Arabs in pursuit. The archbishop bade them turn instantly into a deserted castle they were just passing, to drop the portcullis and man the walls. That they might look as numerous as possible, he bade all the women dress themselves like men and tie their long hair beneath their chins to resemble beards. He then put helmets on their heads and lances in their hands, and thus the Arab leader saw a formidable host on the walls to be besieged. In obedience, perhaps, to orders, he rode away and after sufficient time had passed, the archbishop's party rode onward towards their place of embarkation. Luis found himself beside a dark-eyed maiden, who ambled along on a white mule, and when he ventured to joke her a little on her late appearance as an armed cavalier, she said coyly, " Did you think my only weapons were roses?" Looking

eagerly at her, he recognized the laughing face
which he had once seen at a window; but ere
he could speak again she had struck her mule
lightly and taken refuge beside the archbishop,
where Luis dared not venture.    He did not
recognize the maiden again till they met on
board one of the vessels which the Arabs had
left at Gibraltar, and on which they embarked for
certain islands of which Oppas had heard, which
lay in the Sea of Darkness.    Among these
islands they were to find their future home.

The voyage, at first rough, soon became
serene and quiet; the skies were clear, the
moon shone; the veils of the Spanish maidens
were convenient by day and useless at evening, and Luis had many a low-voiced talk on
the quarter-deck with Juanita, who proved to
be a young relative of the archbishop.    It was
understood that she was to take the veil, and
that, young as she was, she would become, by
and by, the lady abbess of a nunnery to be
established on the islands; and as her kinsman,
though severe to others, was gentle to her,
she had her own way a good deal — especially

beneath the moon and the stars. For the rest, they had daily services of religion, as dignified and sonorous as could have taken place on shore, except on those rare occasions when the chief bass voice was hushed in seasickness in some cabin below. Beautiful Gregorian masses rose to heaven, and it is certain that the Pilgrim fathers, in their two months on the Atlantic, almost a thousand years later, had no such rich melody as floated across those summer seas. Luis was a favorite of Oppas, the archbishop, who never seemed to recognize any danger in having an enamoured youth so near to the demure future abbess. He consulted the youth about many plans. Their aim, it seemed, was the great island called Antillia, as yet unexplored, but reputed to be large enough for many thousand people. Oppas was to organize the chief settlement, and he planned to divide the island into seven dioceses, each bishop having a permanent colony. Once established, they would trade with Spain, and whether it remained Moorish or became Christian, Oppas was sure of friendly relations.

The priests were divided among the three vessels, and among them there was that occasional jarring from which even holy men are not quite free. The different bishops had their partisans, but none dared openly face the imperial Oppas. His supposed favorite Luis was less formidable; he was watched and spied upon, while his devotion to the dignified Juanita was apparent to all. Yet he was always ready to leave her side when Oppas called, and then they discussed together the future prospects of the party: when they should see land, whether it would really be Antillia, whether they should have a good landfall, whether the island would be fertile, whether there would be native inhabitants, and if so, whether they should be baptized and sent to Spain as slaves, or whether they should be retained on the island. It was decided, on the whole, that this last should be done; and what with the prospect of winning souls, and the certainty of having obedient subjects, the prospect seemed inviting.

One morning, at sunrise, there lay before

them a tropic island, soft and graceful, with green shrubs and cocoanut trees, and rising in the distance to mountains whose scooped tops and dark, furrowed sides spoke of extinct volcanoes — yet not so extinct but that a faint wreath of vapor still mounted from the utmost peak of the highest among them.   Here and there were seen huts covered with great leaves or sheaves of grass, and among these they saw figures moving and disappearing, watching their approach, yet always ready to disappear in the recesses of the woods.   Sounding carefully the depth of water with their imperfect tackle, they anchored off the main beach, and sent a boat on shore from each vessel, Luis being in command of one.   The natives at first hovered in the distance, but presently came down to the shore to meet the visitors, some even swimming off to the boats in advance.   They were of a yellow complexion, with good features, were naked except for goat-skins or woven palm fibres, or reeds painted in different colors; and were gay and merry, singing and dancing among themselves.   When brought on board the

ships, they ate bread and figs, but refused wine
and spices; and they seemed not to know
the use of rings or of swords, when shown to
them. Whatever was given to them they
divided with one another. They cultivated
fruit and grain on their island, reared goats,
and seemed willing to share all with their
newly found friends. Luis, always thought-
ful, and somewhat anxious in temperament,
felt many doubts as to the usage which
these peaceful islanders would receive from the
ships' company, no matter how many bishops
and holy men might be on board.

All that day there was exploring by small
companies, and on the next the archbishop
landed in solemn procession. The boats from
the ships all met at early morning, near the
shore, the sight bringing together a crowd of
islanders on the banks; men, women, and children, who, with an instinct that something
of importance was to happen, decked themselves with flowers, wreaths, and plumes, the
number increasing constantly and the crowd
growing more and more picturesque. Forming

from the boats, a procession marched slowly up
the beach, beginning with a few lay brethren,
carrying tools for digging; then acolytes bearing
tall crosses; and then white-robed priests;
the seven bishops being carried on litters, the
archbishop most conspicuously of all. Solemn
chants were sung as the procession moved
through the calm water towards the placid shore,
and the gentle savages joined in kneeling while
a solemn mass was said, and the crosses were
uplifted which took possession of the new-
found land in the name of the Church.

These solemn services occupied much of the
day; later they carried tents on shore, and some
of them occupied large storehouses which the
natives had built for drying their figs; and to
the women, under direction of Juanita, was
allotted a great airy cave, with smaller caves
branching from it, where the natives had made
palm baskets. Day after day they labored,
transferring all their goods and provisions to
the land,—tools, and horses, and mules, clothing,
and simple furniture. Most of them joined with
pleasure in this toil, but others grew restless

M

as they transferred all their possessions to land, and sometimes the women especially would climb to high places and gaze longingly towards Spain.

One morning a surprise came to Luis. Every night it was their custom to have a great fire on the beach, and to meet and sing chants around it. One night Luis had personally put out the blaze of the fire, as it was more windy than usual, and went to sleep in his tent. Soon after midnight he was awakened by a glare of a great light upon his tent's thin walls, and hastily springing up, he saw their largest caravel on fire. Rushing out to give the alarm, he saw a similar flame kindled in the second vessel, and then, after some delay, in the third. Then he saw a dark boat pulling hastily towards the shore, and going down to the beach he met their most trusty captain, who told him that the ships had been burnt by order of the archbishop, in order that their return might be hopeless, and that their stay on the island might be forever.

There was some lamentation among the emigrants when they saw their retreat thus cut off, but Luis when once established on shore did not share it ; to be near Juanita was enough for him, though he rarely saw her.   He began sometimes to feel that the full confidence of the archbishop was withdrawn from him, but he was still high in office, and he rode with Oppas over the great island, marking it out by slow degrees into seven divisions, that each bishop might have a diocese and a city of his own.   Soon the foundations began to be laid, and houses and churches began to be built, for the soft volcanic rock was easily worked, though not very solid for building.   The spot for the cathedral was selected with the unerring eye for a fine situation which the Roman Catholic Church has always shown, and the adjoining convent claimed, as it rose, the care of Juanita.   As general superintendent of the works, it was the duty of Luis sometimes to be in that neighborhood, until one unlucky day when the two lovers, lingering to watch the full moon rise, were interrupted by one of the younger bishops, a black-browed Spaniard of stealthy ways, who had before now taken it upon himself to watch them.   Nothing could be more innocent than their dawning loves, yet how could any love be held innocent on the part of a maiden who was the kinswoman of an archbishop and was his destined choice for the duties of an abbess? The fact that she had never yet taken her preliminary vows or given her consent to take them, counted for nothing in the situation; though any experienced lady-superior could have told the archbishop that no maiden could be wisely made an abbess until she had given some signs of having a vocation for a religious life.

From that moment the youthful pair met no more for weeks. It seemed always necessary for Luis to be occupied elsewhere than in the Cathedral city; as the best architect on the island, he was sent here, there, and everywhere; and the six other churches rose with more rapidity because the archbishop preferred to look after his own. The once peaceful natives found themselves a shade less happy when they were required to work all day long as quarrymen or as builders, but it was something, had they but known it, that they were not borne away as slaves, as happened later on other islands to so many of their race.  To Luis they were always loyal for his cheery ways, although there seemed a change in his spirits as time went on.  But an event happened which brought a greater change still.

A Spanish caravel was seen one day, making towards the port and showing signals of distress. Luis, having just then found an excuse for visiting the Cathedral city, was the first to board her and was hailed with joy by the captain.  He was a townsman of the youth's and had given him his first lessons in navigation. He had been bound, it seemed, for the Canary Islands, and had put in for repairs, which needed only a few days in the quiet waters of a sheltered port.  He could tell Luis of his parents, of his home, and that the northern part of Spain, under Arab sway, was humanely governed, and a certain proportion of Christian churches allowed.  In a few days the caravel sailed again at nightfall; but it carried with it two unexpected passengers; the archbishop lost his architect, and the proposed convent lost its unwilling abbess.

From this point both the Island of the Seven Cities and its escaping lovers disappear from all definite records. It was a period when expeditions of discovery came and went, and when one wondrous tale drove out another. There exist legends along the northern coast of Spain in the region of Santander, for instance, of a youth who once eloped with a high-born maiden and came there to dwell, but there may have been many such youths and many such maidens — who knows? Of Antillia itself, or the Island of the Seven Cities, it is well known that it appeared on the maps of the Atlantic, sometimes under the one name and sometimes under another, six hundred years after the date assigned by the story that has here been told. It was said by Fernando Columbus to have been revisited by a Portuguese sailor in 1447; and the name appeared on the globe of Behaim in 1492.

The geographer Toscanelli, in his famous letter to Columbus, recommended Antillia as likely to · be useful to Columbus as a way station for reaching India, and when the great explorer reached Hispaniola, he was supposed to have discovered the mysterious island, whence the name of Antilles was given to the group. Later, the first explorers of New Mexico thought that the pueblos were the Seven Cities; so that both the names of the imaginary island have been preserved, although those of Luis de Vega and his faithful Juanita have not been recorded until the telling of this tale.

# XVI

## HARALD THE VIKING

ERIK THE RED, the most famous of all Vikings, had three sons, and once when they were children the king came to visit Erik and passed through the playground where the boys were playing. Leif and Biorn, the two oldest, were building little houses and barns and were making believe that they were full of cattle and sheep, while Harald, who was only four years old, was sailing chips of wood in a pool. The king asked Harald what they were, and he said, "Ships of war." King Olaf laughed and said, "The time may come when you will command ships, my little friend." Then he asked Biorn what he would like best to have. "Cornland," he said; "ten farms." "That would yield much corn," the king replied. Then he asked Leif the same question, and he answered, "Cows." "How many?" "So many that when they went to the lake to be watered, they would stand close round the edge, so that not another could pass." "That would be a large housekeeping," said the king, and he asked the same question of Harald. "What would you like best to have?" "Servants and followers," said the child, stoutly. "How many would you like?" "Enough," said the child, "to eat up all the cows and crops of my brothers at a single meal." Then the king laughed, and said to the mother of the children, "You are bringing up a king."

As the boys grew, Leif and Harald were ever fond of roaming, while Biorn wished to live on the farm at peace. Their sister Freydis went with the older boys and urged them on. She was not gentle and amiable, but full of energy and courage: she was also quarrelsome and vindictive. People said of her that even if her brothers were all killed, yet the race of Erik the Red would not end while she lived; that "she practised more of shooting and the handling of sword and shield than of sewing or embroidering, and that as she was able, she did evil oftener than good; and that when she was hindered she ran into the woods and slew men to get their property." She was always urging her brothers to deeds of daring and adventure. One day they had been hawking, and when they let slip the falcons, Harald's falcon killed two blackcocks in one flight and three in another. The dogs ran and brought the birds, and he said proudly to the others, "It will be long before most of you have any such success," and they all agreed to this. He rode home in high spirits and showed his birds to his sister Freydis. "Did any king," he asked, "ever make so great a capture in so short a time?" "It is, indeed," she said, "a good morning's hunting to have got five blackcocks, but it was still better when in one morning a king of Norway took five kings and subdued all their kingdoms." Then Harald went away very humble and besought his father to let him go and serve on the Varangian Guard of King Otho at Constantinople, that he might learn to be a warrior.

So Harald was brought from his Norwegian home by his father Erik the Red, in his galley called the *Sea-serpent*, and sailed with him through the Mediterranean Sea, and was at last made a member of the Emperor Otho's Varangian Guard at Constantinople. This guard will be well remembered by the readers of Scott's novel, "Count Robert of Paris," and was maintained by successive emperors and drawn largely from the Scandinavian races. Erik the Red had no hesitation in leaving his son among them, as the young man was stout and strong, very self-willed, and quite able to defend himself. The father knew also that the Varangian Guard, though hated by the people, held to one another like a band of brothers; and that any one brought up among them would be sure of plenty of fighting and plenty of gold,— the two things most prized by early Norsemen. For ordinary life, Harald's chief duties would be to lounge about the palace, keeping guard, wearing helmet and buckler and bearskin, with purple under-clothes and golden clasped hose; and bearing as armor a mighty battle-axe and a small scimitar. Such was the life led by Harald, till one day he had a message from his father, through a new

recruit, calling him home to join an expedition
to the western seas. " I hear, my son," the
message said, "that your good emperor, whom
may the gods preserve, is sorely ill and may die
any day. When he is dead, be prompt in
getting your share of the plunder of the palace
and come back to me."

The emperor died, and the order was fulfilled.
It was the custom of the Varangians to reward
themselves in this way for their faithful services
of protection ; and the result is that, to this day,
Greek and Arabic gold crosses and chains are to
be found in the houses of Norwegian peasants
and may be seen in the museums of Christiania
and Copenhagen. No one was esteemed the
less for this love of spoil, if he was only generous
in giving. The Norsemen spoke contempt-
uously of gold as " the serpent's bed," and
called a generous man " a hater of the serpent's
bed," because such a man parts with gold as with
a thing he hates.

When the youth came to his father, he found
Erik the Red directing the building of one of
the great Norse galleys, nearly eighty feet long

and seventeen wide and only six feet deep. The boat had twenty ribs, and the frame was fastened together by withes made of roots, while the oaken planks were held by iron rivets. The oars were twenty feet long, and were put through oar holes, and the rudder, shaped like a large oar, was not at the end, but was attached to a projecting beam on the starboard (originally steer-board) side. The ship was to be called a Dragon, and was to be painted so as to look like one, having a gilded dragon's head at the bow and a gilded tail on the stern; while the moving oars would look like legs, and the row of red and white shields, hung along the side of the boat, would resemble the scales of a dragon, and the great square sails, red and blue, would look like wings. This was the vessel which young Harald was to command.

He had already made trips in just such vessels with his father; had learned to attack the enemy with arrow and spear; also with stones thrown down from above, and with grappling-irons to clutch opposing boats. He had learned to swim, from early childhood, even in the icy northern

waters, and he had been trained in swimming to
hide his head beneath his floating shield, so
that it could not be seen. He had learned also
to carry tinder in a walnut shell, enclosed in wax,
so that no matter how long he had been in the
water he could strike a light on reaching shore.
He had also learned from his father acts of escape
as well as attack. Thus he had once sailed on a
return trip from Denmark after plundering a
town; the ships had been lying at anchor all
night in a fog, and at sunlight in the morning
lights seemed burning on the sea. But Erik
the Red said, " It is a fleet of Danish ships, and
the sun strikes on the gilded dragon crests; furl
the sail and take to the oars." They rowed
their best, yet the Danish ships were overtaking
them, when Erik the Red ordered his men to
throw wood overboard and cover it with Danish
plunder. This made some delay, as the Danes
stopped to pick it up, and in the same way Erik
the Red dropped his provisions, and finally his
prisoners; and in the delay thus caused he got
away with his own men.

But now Harald was not to go to Denmark,

but to the new western world, the Wonder-strands which Leif had sought and had left without sufficient exploration. First, however, he was to call at Greenland, which his father had first discovered. It was the custom of the Viking explorers, when they reached a new country, to throw overboard their "seat posts," or *setstokka*, — the curved part of their doorways, — and then to land where they floated ashore. But Erik the Red had lent his to a friend and could not get them back, so that he sailed in search of them, and came to a new land which he called Greenland, because, as he said, people would be attracted thither if it had a good name. Then he established a colony there, and then Leif the Lucky, as he was called, sailed still farther, and came to the Wonderstrand, or Magic Shores. These he called Vinland or Wine-land, and now a rich man named Karlsefne was to send a colony thither from Greenland, and the young Harald was to go with it and take command of it.

Now as Harald was to be presented to the rich Karlsefne, he thought he must be gorgeously arrayed. So he wore a helmet on his head, a red

shield richly inlaid with gold and iron, and a
sharp sword with an ivory handle wound with
golden thread. He had also a short spear, and
wore over his coat a red silk short cloak on which
was embroidered, both before and behind, a yellow lion. We may well believe that the sixty
men and five women who composed the expedition were ready to look on him with admiration, especially as one of the women was his own
sister, Freydis, now left to his peculiar care, since
Erik the Red had died. The sturdy old hero
had died still a heathen, and it was only just
after his death that Christianity was introduced
into Greenland, and those numerous churches
were built there whose ruins yet remain, even in
regions from which all population has gone.

So the party of colonists sailed for Vinland,
and Freydis, with the four older women, came in
Harald's boat, and Freydis took easily the lead
among them for strength, though not always, it
must be admitted, for amiability.

The boats of the expedition having left Greenland soon after the year 1000, coasted the shore
as far as they could, rarely venturing into open

sea. At last, amidst fog and chilly weather, they made land at a point where a river ran through a lake into the sea, and they could not enter from the sea except at high tide. It was once believed that this was Narragansett Bay in Rhode Island, but this is no longer believed. Here they landed and called the place Hóp, from the Icelandic word *hópa*, meaning an inlet from the ocean. Here they found grape-vines growing and fields of wild wheat; there were fish in the lake and wild animals in the woods. Here they landed the cattle and the provisions which they had brought with them; and here they built their huts. They went in the spring, and during that summer the natives came in boats of skin to trade with them — men described as black, and ill favored, with large eyes and broad cheeks and with coarse hair on their heads. These, it is thought, may have been the Esquimaux. The first time they came, these visitors held up a white shield as a sign of peace, and were so frightened by the bellowing of the bull that they ran away. Then returning, they brought

N

furs to sell and wished to buy weapons, but
Harald tried another plan: he bade the women
bring out milk, butter, and cheese from their
dairies, and when the Skrælings saw that, they
wished for nothing else, and, the legend says,
"the Skrælings carried away their wares in
their stomachs, but the Norsemen had the
skins they had purchased." This happened yet
again, but at the second visit one of the Skrælings was accidentally killed or injured.

The next time the Skrælings came they were
armed with slings, and raised upon a pole a
great blue ball and attacked the Norsemen so
furiously that they were running away when
Erik's sister, Freydis, came out before them
with bare arms, and took up a sword, saying,
"Why do you run, strong men as you are,
from these miserable dwarfs whom I thought
you would knock down like cattle? Give me
weapons, and I will fight better than any of
you." Then the rest took courage and began
to fight, and the Skrælings were driven back.
Once more the strangers came, and one of
them took up an axe, a thing which he had

not before seen, and struck at one of his companions, killing him. Then the leader took the axe and threw it into the water, after which the Skrælings retreated, and were not seen again.

The winter was a mild one, and while it lasted, the Norsemen worked busily at felling wood and house-building. They had also many amusements, in most of which Harald excelled. They used to swim in all weathers. One of their feats was to catch seals and sit on them while swimming; another was to pull one another down and remain as long as possible under water. Harald could swim for a mile or more with his armor on, or with a companion on his shoulder. In-doors they used to play the tug of war, dragging each other by a walrus hide across the fire. Harald was good at this, and was also the best archer, sometimes aiming at something placed on a boy's head, the boy having a cloth tied around his head, and held by two men, that he might not move at all on hearing the whistling of the arrow. In this way Harald could even shoot an

arrow under a nut placed on the head, so
that the nut would roll down and the head not
be hurt. He could plant a spear in the
ground and then shoot an arrow upward so
skilfully that it would turn in the air and
fall with the point in the end of the spear-
shaft. He could also shoot a blunt arrow
through the thickest ox-hide from a cross-bow.
He could change weapons from one hand to
the other during a fencing match, or fence with
either hand, or throw two spears at the same
time, or catch a spear in motion. He could
run so fast that no horse could overtake him,
and play the rough games with bat and ball,
using a ball of the hardest wood. He could
race on snowshoes, or wrestle when bound by
a belt to his antagonist. Then when he and
his companions wished a rest, they amused
themselves with harp-playing or riddles or chess.
The Norsemen even played chess on board
their vessels, and there are still to be seen, on
some of these, the little holes that were formerly used for the sharp ends of the chessmen,
so that they should not be displaced.

They could not find that any European had ever visited this place; but some of the Skrælings told them of a place farther south, which they called "the Land of the Whiteman," or "Great Ireland." They said that in that place there were white men who clothed themselves in long white garments, carried before them poles to which white cloths were hung, and called with a loud voice. These, it was thought by the Norsemen, must be Christian processions, in which banners were borne and hymns were chanted. It has been thought from this that some expedition from Ireland — that of St. Brandan, for instance — may have left a settlement there, long before, but this has never been confirmed. The Skrælings and the Northmen were good friends for a time; until at last one of Erik's own warriors killed a Skræling by accident, and then all harmony was at an end.

They saw no hope of making a lasting settlement there, and, moreover, Freydis who was very grasping, tried to deceive the other settlers and get more than her share of everything, so that Harald himself lost patience with her and threat-

ened her.   It happened that one of the men of
the party, Olaf, was Harald's foster-brother.
They had once had a fight, and after the battle
had agreed that they would be friends for life
and always share the same danger.   For this vow
they were to walk under the turf; that is, a strip
of turf was cut and held above their heads, and
they stood beneath and let their blood flow upon
the ground whence the turf had been cut.   After
this they were to own everything by halves and
either must avenge the other's death.   This was
their brotherhood; but Freydis did not like it; so
she threatened Olaf, and tried to induce men to
kill him, for she did not wish to bring upon herself the revenge that must come if she slew him.

This was the reason why the whole enterprise
failed, and why Olaf persuaded Harald, for the
sake of peace, to return to Greenland in the
spring and take a load of valuable timber to sell
there, including one stick of what was called
massur-wood, which was as valuable as ma-
hogany, and may have been at some time borne
by ocean currents to the beach.   It is hardly
possible that, as some have thought, the colo-

nists established a regular trade in this wood for
no such wood grows on the northern Atlantic
shores. However this may be, the party soon
returned, after one winter in Vinland the Good;
and on the way back Harald did one thing which
made him especially dear to his men.

A favorite feat of the Norsemen was to toss
three swords in the air and catch each by the
handle as it came down. This was called the
*handsax* game. The young men used also to try
the feat of running along the oar-blades of the
rowers as they were in motion, passing around
the bow of the vessel with a spring and coming
round to the stern over the oars on the other
side. Few could accomplish this, but no one but
Harald could do it and play the *handsax* game
as he ran; and when he did it, they all said that
he was the most skilful man at *idrottie* ever seen.
That was their word for an athletic feat. But
presently came a time when not only his courage
but his fairness and justice were to be tried.

It happened in this way. There was nothing
of which the Norsemen were more afraid than of
the *teredo*, or shipworm, which gnaws the wood

of ships.　It was observed in Greenland and Iceland that pieces of wood often floated on shore which were filled with holes made by this animal, and they thought that in certain places the seas were full of this worm, so that a ship would be bored and sunk in a little while.　It is said that on this return voyage Harald's vessel entered a worm-sea and presently began to sink.　They had, however, provided a smaller boat smeared with sea-oil, which the worms would not attack. They went into the boat, but found that it would not hold more than half of them all.　Then Harald said, "We will divide by lots, without regard to the rank; each taking his chance with the rest."　This they thought, the Norse legend says, "a high-minded offer."　They drew lots, and Harald was among those assigned to the safer boat.　He stepped in, and when he was there a man called from the other boat and said, "Dost thou intend, Harald, to separate from me here?" Harald answered, "So it turns out," and the man said, "Very different was thy promise to my father when we came from Greenland, for the promise was that we should share the same fate."

Then Harald said, "It shall not be thus. Go into the boat, and I will go back into the ship, since thou art so anxious to live." Then Harald went back to the ship, while the man took his place in the boat, and after that Harald was never heard of more.

# XVII

## THE SEARCH FOR NORUMBEGA

SIR HUMPHREY GILBERT, colonel of the British forces in the Netherlands, was poring over the manuscript narrative of David Ingram, mariner. Ingram had in 1568–69 taken the widest range of travel that had ever been taken in the new continent, of which it was still held doubtful by many whether it was or was not a part of Asia. "Surely," Gilbert said to his half-brother, Walter Raleigh, a youth of twenty-three, "this knave hath seen strange things. He hath been set ashore by John Hawkins in the Gulf of Mexico and there left behind. He hath travelled northward with two of his companions along Indian trails; he hath even reached Norumbega; he hath seen that famous city with its houses of crystal and silver."

"Pine logs and hemlock bark, belike," said Raleigh, scornfully.

"Nay," said Gilbert, "he hath carefully written it down. He saw kings decorated with rubies six inches long; and they were borne on chairs of silver and crystal, adorned with precious stones. He saw pearls as common as pebbles, and the natives were laden down by their ornaments of gold and silver. The city of Bega was three-quarters of a mile long and had many streets wider than those of London. Some houses had massive pillars of crystal and silver."

"What assurance can he give?" asked Raleigh.

"He offers on his life to prove it."

"A small offer, mayhap. There be many of these lying mariners whose lives are as worthless as the stories they relate. But what said he of the natives?"

"Kindly disposed," was the reply, "so far as he went, but those dwelling farther north, where he did not go, were said to be cannibals with teeth like those of dogs, whereby you may know them."

"Travellers' tales," said Raleigh. "*Omne ignotum pro mirifico.*"

"He returned," said Gilbert, disregarding the

interruption, "in the *Gargarine*, a French vessel commanded by Captain Champagne."

"Methinks something of the flavor represented by the good captain's name hath got into your Englishman's brain. Good ale never gives such fantasies. Doth he perchance speak of elephants?"

"He doth," said Sir Humphrey, hesitatingly. "Perchance he saw them not, but heard of them only."

"What says he of them?" asked Raleigh.

"He says that he saw in that country both elephants and ounces; and he says that their trumpets are made of elephants' teeth."

"But the houses," said Raleigh; "tell me of the houses."

"In every house," said Gilbert, reading from the manuscript, "they have scoops, buckets, and divers vessels, all of massive silver with which they throw out water and otherwise employ them. The women wear great plates of gold covering their bodies, and chains of great pearls in the manner of curvettes; and the men wear manilions

or bracelets on each arm and each leg, some of
gold and some of silver."

" Whence come they, these gauds?"

"There are great rivers where one may find
pieces of gold as big as the fist; and there are
great rocks of crystal, sufficient to load many
ships."

This was all which was said on that day, but
never was explorer more eager than Gilbert.  He
wrote a " Discourse of a Discoverie for a New
Passage to Cathaia and the East Indies " — published without his knowledge by George Gas-
coigne.  In 1578 he had from Queen Elizabeth
a patent of exploration, allowing him to take
possession of any uncolonized lands in North
America, paying for these a fifth of all gold and
silver found.  The next year he sailed with Raleigh for Newfoundland, but one vessel was lost
and the others returned to England.  In 1583,
he sailed again, taking with him the narrative of
Ingram, which he reprinted.  He also took with
him a learned Hungarian from Buda, named
Parmenius, who went for the express purpose of
singing the praise of Norumbega in Latin verse,

but was drowned in Sir Humphrey's great flag-ship, the *Delight*. This wreck took place near Sable Island, and as most of the supplies for the expedition went down in the flag-ship, the men in the remaining vessels grew so impatient as to compel a return. There were two vessels, the *Golden Hind* of forty tons, and the *Squirrel* of ten tons, this last being a mere boat then called a frigate, a small vessel propelled by both sails and oars, quite unlike the war-ship afterwards called by that name. On both these vessels the men were so distressed that they gathered on the bulwarks, pointing to their empty mouths and their ragged clothing. The officers of the *Golden Hind* were unwilling to return, but consented on Sir Humphrey's promise that they should come back in the spring; they sailed for England on the 31st of August. All wished him to return in the *Golden Hind* as a much larger and safer vessel; the *Squirrel*, besides its smallness, being encumbered on the deck with guns, ammunition, and nettings, making it unseaworthy. But when he was begged to remove into the larger vessel, he said, " I will not forsake my little company going

homeward with whom I have passed so many
storms and perils." One reason for this was, the
narrator of the voyage says, because of "hard re-
ports given of him that he was afraid of the sea,
albeit this was rather rashness than advised resolution, to prefer the wind of a vain report to
the weight of his own life."

On the very day of sailing they caught their
first glimpse of some large species of seal or
walrus, which is thus described by the old narrator of the expedition:—

"So vpon Saturday in the afternoone the
31 of August, we changed our course, and
returned backe for England, at which very
instant, euen in winding about, there passed
along betweene vs and towards the land which
we now forsooke a very lion to our seeming,
in shape, hair and colour, not swimming after
the maner of a beast by moouing of his feete,
but rather sliding vpon the water with his whole
body (excepting the legs) in sight, neither yet
in diuing vnder, and againe rising aboue the
water, as the maner is, of Whales, Dolphins,
Tunise, Porposes, and all other fish: but con-

fidently shewing himselfe aboue water without hiding: Notwithstanding, we presented our selues in open view and gesture to amase him, as all creatures will be commonly at a sudden gaze and sight of men. Thus he passed along turning his head to and fro, yawning and gaping wide, with ougly demonstration of long teeth, and glaring eies, and to bidde vs a farewell (comming right against the Hinde) he sent forth a horrible voyce, roaring or bellowing as doeth a lion, which spectacle wee all beheld so farre as we were able to discerne the same, as men prone to wonder at euery strange thing, as this doubtlesse was, to see a lion in the Ocean sea, or fish in shape of a lion. What opinion others had thereof, and chiefly the Generall himselfe, I forbeare to deliuer: But he tooke it for Bonum Omen [a good omen], reioycing that he was to warre against such an enemie, if it were the deuill."

When they came north of the Azores, very violent storms met them; most "outrageous seas," the narrator says; and they saw little lights upon the mainyard called then by sailors "Castor and Pollux," and now "St. Elmo's Fire"; yet they had but one of these at a time, and this is thought a sign of tempest. On September 9, in the afternoon, "the general," as they called him, Sir Humphrey, was sitting abaft with a book in his hand, and cried out more than once to those in the other vessel, "We are as near to heaven by sea as by land." And that same night about twelve o'clock, the frigate being ahead of the *Golden Hind*, the lights of the smaller vessel suddenly disappeared, and they knew that she had sunk in the sea. The event is well described in a ballad by Longfellow.

The name of Norumbega and the tradition of its glories survived Sir Humphrey Gilbert. In a French map of 1543, the town appears with castle and towers. Jean Allfonsce, who visited New England in that year, describes it as the capital of a great fur country. Students of Indian tongues defined the word as meaning "the place of a fine city"; while the learned Grotius seized upon it as being the same as

o

Norberga and so affording a relic of the visits of the Northmen. As to the locality, it appeared first on the maps as a large island, then as a smaller one, and after 1569 no longer as an island, but a part of the mainland, bordering apparently on the Penobscot River. Whittier in his poem of " Norumbega " describes a Norman knight as seeking it in vain.

> " He turned him back, ' O master dear,
>     We are but men misled;
>   And thou hast sought a city here
>     To find a grave instead.
>
> \*     \*     \*     \*     \*     \*
>
> " ' No builded wonder of these lands
>     My weary eyes shall see;
>   A city never made with hands
>     Alone awaiteth me.' "

So Champlain, in 1604, could find no trace of it, and said that " no such marvel existed," while Mark Lescarbot, the Parisian advocate, writing in 1609, says, " If this beautiful town ever existed in nature, I would like to know who pulled it down, for there is nothing here

but huts made of pickets and covered with the
barks of trees or skins." Yet it kept its place
on maps till 1640, and even Heylin in his
" Cosmography " (1669) speaks of " Norumbega
and its fair city," though he fears that the
latter never existed.

It is a curious fact that the late Mr. Justin
Winsor, the eminent historian, after much inquiry
among the present descendants of the Indian
tribes in Maine, could never find any one who
could remember to have heard the name of
Norumbega.

# XVIII

## THE GUARDIANS OF THE ST. LAWRENCE

WHEN in 1611 the Sieur de Champlain went back to France to report his wonderful explorations in Canada, he was soon followed by a young Frenchman named Vignan, who had spent a whole winter among the Indians, in a village where there was no other white man. This was a method often adopted by the French for getting more knowledge of Indian ways and commanding their confidence. Vignan had made himself a welcome guest in the cabins, and had brought away many of their legends, to which he added some of his own. In particular, he declared that he had penetrated into the interior until he had come upon a great lake of salt water, far to the northwest. This was, as it happened, the very thing which the French government and all Europe had most hoped to find. They

had always believed that sooner or later a
short cut would be discovered across the newly
found continent, a passage leading to the Pacific Ocean and far Cathay. This was the
dream of all French explorers, and of Champlain in particular, and his interest was at once
excited by anything that looked toward the
Pacific. Now Vignan had prepared himself
with just the needed information. He said
that during his winter with the Indians he had
made the very discovery needed; that he had
ascended the river Ottawa, which led to a
body of salt water so large that it seemed
like an ocean; that he had just seen on its
shores the wreck of an English ship, from
which eighty men had been taken and slain
by the savages, and that they had with them
an English boy whom they were keeping to
present to Champlain.

This tale about the English ship was evidently
founded on the recent calamities of Henry
Hudson, of which Vignan had heard some garbled
account, and which he used as coloring for his
story. The result was that Champlain was thor-

oughly interested in the tale, and that Vignan
was cross-examined and tested, and was made at
last to certify to the truth of it before two nota-
ries of Rochelle.   Champlain privately consulted
the chancellor de Sillery, the old Marquis de
Brissac, and others, who all assured him that
the matter should be followed up; and he resolved to make it the subject of an exploration
without delay.   He sailed in one vessel, and
Vignan in another, the latter taking with him
an ardent young Frenchman, Albert de Brissac.

M. de Vignan, talking with the young Brissac
on the voyage, told him wonderful tales of
monsters which were, he said, the guardians of
the St. Lawrence River.   There was, he said, an
island in the bay of Chaleurs, near the mouth of
that river, where a creature dwelt, having the
form of a woman and called by the Indians
Gougou.   She was very frightful, and so enormous that the masts of the vessel could not reach
her waist.   She had already eaten many savages
and constantly continued to do so, putting them
first into a great pocket to await her hunger.
Some of those who had escaped said that this

pocket was large enough to hold a whole ship. This creature habitually made dreadful noises, and several savages who came on board claimed to have heard them.   A man from St. Malo in France, the Sieur de Prevert, confirmed this story, and said that he had passed so near the den of this frightful being, that all on board could hear its hissing, and all hid themselves below, lest it should carry them off.   This naturally made much impression upon the young Sieur de Brissac, and he doubtless wished many times that he had stayed at home.   On the other hand, he observed that both M. de Vignan and M. de Prevert took the tale very coolly and that there seemed no reason why he should distrust himself if they did not.   Yet he was very glad when, after passing many islands and narrow straits, the river broadened and they found themselves fairly in the St. Lawrence and past the haunted Bay of Chaleurs.   They certainly heard a roaring and a hissing in the distance, but it may have been the waves on the beach.

But this was not their last glimpse of the supposed guardians of the St. Lawrence.   As the ship proceeded farther up the beautiful river, they saw one morning a boat come forth from the woods, bearing three men dressed to look like devils, wrapped in dogs' skins, white and black, their faces besmeared as black as any coals, with horns on their heads more than a yard long, and as this boat passed the ship, one of the men made a long address, not looking towards them. Then they all three fell flat in the boat, when Indians rowed out to meet them and guided them to a landing.

Then many Indians collected in the woods and began a loud talk which they could hear on board the ships and which lasted half an hour. Then two of their leaders came towards the shore, holding their hands upward joined together, and meanwhile carrying their hats under their upper garments and showing great reverence. Looking upward they sometimes cried, "Jesus, Jesus," or "Jesus Maria." Then the captain asked them whether anything ill had happened, and they said in French, "Nenni est il bon," meaning that it was not good. Then they said that their god Cudraigny had spoken in

Hochelaga (Montreal) and had sent these three men to show to them that there was so much snow and ice in the country that he who went there would die.   This made the Frenchmen laugh, saying in reply that their god Cudraigny was but a fool and a noddy and knew not what he said.   " Tell him," said a Frenchman, " that Christ will defend them from all cold, if they will believe in him."   The Indians then asked the captain if he had spoken with Jesus.   He answered No; but that his priests had, and they had promised fair weather.   Hearing this, they thanked the captain and told the other Indians in the woods, who all came rushing out, seeming to be very glad.   Giving great shouts, they began to sing and dance as they had done before. They also began to bring to the ships great stores of fish and of bread made of millet, casting it into the French boats so thickly that it seemed to fall from heaven.   Then the Frenchmen went on shore, and the people came clustering about them, bringing children in their arms to be touched, as if to hallow them.   Then the captain in return arranged the women in order and gave them beads made of tin, and other trifles, and gave knives to the men. All that night the Indians made great fires and danced and sang along the shore. But when the Frenchmen had finally reached the mouth of the Ottawa and had begun to ascend it, under Vignan's guidance, they had reasons to remember the threats of the god Cudraigny.

Ascending the Ottawa in canoes, past cataracts, boulders, and precipices, they at last, with great labor, reached the island of Allumette, at a distance of two hundred and twenty-five miles. Often it was impossible to carry their canoes past waterfalls, because the forests were so dense, so that they had to drag the boats by ropes, wading among rocks or climbing along precipices. Gradually they left behind them their armor, their provisions, and clothing, keeping only their canoes; they lived on fish and wild fowl, and were sometimes twenty-four hours without food. Champlain himself carried three French arquebuses or short guns, three oars, his cloak, and many smaller articles; and was harassed by dense clouds of mosquitoes all the time. Vignan, Brissac, and the rest were almost as heavily loaded. The tribe of Indians whom they at last reached had chosen the spot as being inaccessible to their enemies; and thought that the newcomers had fallen from the clouds.

When Champlain inquired after the salt sea promised by Vignan, he learned to his indignation that the whole tale was false. Vignan had spent a winter at the very village where they were, but confessed that he had never gone a league further north. The Indians knew of no such sea, and craved permission to torture and kill him for his deceptions; they called him loudly a liar, and even the children took up the cry and jeered at him. They said, " Do you not see that he meant to cause your death? Give him to us, and we promise you that he shall not lie any more." Champlain defended him from their attacks, bore it all philosophically, and the young Brissac went back to France, having given up hope of reaching the salt sea, except, as Champlain himself coolly said, " in imagination." The guardians of the St. Lawrence had at least exerted their spell to the extent of saying, Thus far and no farther. Vignan never admitted that he had invented the story of the Gougou, and had bribed the Indians who acted the part of devils, — and perhaps he did not, — but it is certain that neither the giantess nor the god Cudraigny has ever again been heard from.

# XIX

## THE ISLAND OF DEMONS

THOSE American travellers who linger with delight among the narrow lanes and picturesque, overhanging roofs of Honfleur, do not know what a strange tragedy took place on a voyage which began in that quaint old port three centuries and a half ago. When, in 1536, the Breton sailor Jacques Cartier returned from his early explorations of the St. Lawrence, which he had ascended as high as Hochelaga, King Francis I. sent for him at the lofty old house known as the House of the Salamander, in a narrow street of the quaint town of Lisieux. It now seems incredible that the most powerful king in Europe should have dwelt in such a meagre lane, yet the house still stands there as a witness; although a visitor must now brush away the rough, ready-made garments and fishermen's overalls which overhang its door. Over that stairway, nevertheless, the troubadours, Pierre Ronsard and Clement Marot, used to go up and down, humming their lays or touching their viols; and through that door De Lorge returned in glory, after leaping down into the lions' den to rescue his lady's glove. The house still derives its name from the great carved image of a reptile which stretches down its outer wall, from garret to cellar, beside the doorway.

In that house the great king deigned to meet the Breton sailor, who had set up along the St. Lawrence a cross bearing the arms of France with the inscription *Franciscus Primus, Dei gratia Francorum Rex regnat;* and had followed up the pious act by kidnapping the king Donnacona, and carrying him back to France. This savage potentate was himself brought to Lisieux to see his French fellow-sovereign; and the jovial king, eagerly convinced, decided to send Cartier forth again, to explore for other wonders, and perhaps bring back other kingly brethren. Meanwhile, however, as it was get-

ting to be an affair of royalty, he decided to
send also a gentleman of higher grade than a
pilot, and so selected Jean Françoìs de la
Roche, Sieur de Roberval, whom he commissioned as lieutenant and governor of Canada
and Hochelaga. Roberval was a gentleman
of credit and renown in Picardy, and was sometimes jocosely called by Francis "the little king
of Vimeu." He was commissioned at Fon-
tainebleau, and proceeded to superintend the
building of ships at St. Malo.

Marguerite Roberval, his fair-haired and
black-eyed niece, was to go with him on the
voyage, with other ladies of high birth, and
also with the widowed Madame de Noailles,
her *gouvernante*. Roberval himself remained at
St. Malo to superintend the building of the
ships, and Marguerite and her *gouvernante* would
sit for hours in a beautiful nook by the ship-
yards, where they could overlook the vessels in
rapid construction, or else watch the wondrous
swirl of the tide as it swept in and out, leaving
the harbor bare at low tide, but with eight fathoms of water when the tide was full. The de-

signer of the ships often came, cap in hand, to ask or answer questions — one of those frank and manly French fishermen and pilots, whom the French novelists describe as "*un solide gaillard*," or such as Victor Hugo paints in his "Les Travailleurs de la Mer." The son of a notary, Etienne Gosselin was better educated than most of the young noblemen whom Marguerite knew, and only his passion for the sea and for nautical construction had kept him a shipbuilder. No wonder that the young Marguerite, who had led the sheltered life of the French maiden, was attracted by his manly look, his open face, his merry blue eyes, and curly hair. There was about her a tinge of romance, which made her heart an easier thing to reach for such a lover than for one within her own grade ; and as the voyage itself was a world of romance, a little more or less of the romantic was an easy thing to add. Meanwhile Madame de Noailles read her breviary and told her beads and took little naps, wholly ignorant of the drama that was beginning its perilous unfolding before her. When the Sieur de Roberval

returned, the shipbuilder became a mere shipbuilder again.

Three tall ships sailed from Honfleur on August 22, 1541, and on one of them, *La Grande Hermine*, — so called to distinguish it from a smaller
boat of that name, which had previously sailed
with Cartier, — were the Sieur de Roberval, his
niece, and her *gouvernante*. She also had with
her a Huguenot nurse, who had been with her
from a child, and cared for her devotedly. Roberval naturally took with him, for future needs,
the best shipbuilder of St. Malo, Etienne Gosselin. The voyage was long, and there is reason
to think that the Sieur de Roberval was not a
good sailor, while as to the *gouvernante*, she may
have been as helpless as the seasick chaperon of
yachting excursions. Like them, she suffered
the most important events to pass unobserved,
and it was not till too late that she discovered,
what more censorious old ladies on board had
already seen, that her young charge lingered too
often and too long on the quarter-deck when
Etienne Gosselin was planning ships for the
uncle. When she found it out, she was roused

P

to just indignation; but being, after all, but a kindly dowager, with a heart softened by much reading of the interminable tales of Madame de Scudéry, she only remonstrated with Marguerite, wept over her little romance, and threatened to break the sad news to the Sieur de Roberval, yet never did so. Other ladies were less considerate; it all broke suddenly upon the angry uncle; the youth was put in irons, and threatened with flogging, and forbidden to approach the quarter-deck again. But love laughs at locksmiths; Gosselin was relieved of his irons in a day or two because he could not be spared from his work in designing the forthcoming ship, and as both he and Marguerite were of a tolerably determined nature, they invoked, through the old nurse, the aid of a Huguenot minister on board, who had before sailed with Cartier to take charge of the souls of some Protestant vagabonds on the ship, and who was now making a second trip for the same reason. That night, after dark, he joined the lovers in marriage; within twenty-four hours Roberval had heard of it, and had vowed a vengeance quick and sure.

The next morning, under his orders, the vessel lay to under the lee of a rocky island, then known to the sailors as l'Isle des Demons from the fierce winds that raged round it. There was no house there, no living person, no tradition of any; only rocks, sands, and deep forests. With dismay, the ship's company heard that it was the firm purpose of Roberval to put the offending bride on shore, giving her only the old nurse for company, and there to leave her with provisions for three months, trusting to some other vessel to take the exiled women away within that time. The very ladies whose love of scandal had first revealed to him the alleged familiarities, now besought him with many tears to abandon the thought of a doom so terrible. Vainly Madame de Noailles implored mercy for the young girl from a penalty such as was never imposed in any of Madame de Scudéry's romances; vainly the Huguenot minister and the Catholic chaplain, who had fought steadily on questions of doctrine during the whole voyage, now united in appeals for pardon. At least they implored him to let the offenders have a man-servant or two with them to protect them against wild beasts or buccaneers. He utterly refused until, at last wearied out, his wild nature yielded to one of those sudden impulses which were wont to sweep over it; and he exclaimed, " Is it that they need a man-servant, then? Let this insolent caitiff, Gosselin, be relieved of his irons and sent on shore. Let him be my niece's servant or, since a Huguenot marriage is as good as any in the presence of bears and buccaneers, let her call the hound her husband, if she likes. I have done with her; and the race from which she came disowns her forever."

Thus it was done. Etienne was released from his chains and sent on shore. An arquebus and ammunition were given him; and resisting the impulse to send his first shot through the heart of his tyrant, he landed, and the last glimpse seen of the group as the *Grande Hermine* sailed away, was the figure of Marguerite sobbing on his shoulder, and of the unhappy nurse, now somewhat plethoric, and certainly not the person to be selected as a pioneer, sitting upon a rock, weeping profusely. The ship's sails filled, the angry Roberval never looked back on his deserted niece, and the night closed down upon the lonely Isle of Demons, now newly occupied by three unexpected settlers, two of whom at least were happy in each other.

A few boxes of biscuits, a few bottles of wine, had been put on shore with them, enough to feed them for a few weeks. They had brought flint and steel to strike fire, and some ammunition. The chief penalty of the crime did not lie, after all, in the cold and the starvation and the wild beasts and the possible visits of pirates; it lay in the fact that it was the Island of Demons where they were to be left; and in that superstitious age this meant everything that was terrible. For the first few nights of their stay, they fancied that they heard superhuman voices in every wind that blew, every branch that creaked against another branch; and they heard, at any rate, more substantial sounds from the nightly wolves or from the bears which ice-floes had floated to that northern isle. They watched Roberval sail away, he rejoicing, as the old legend of Thevet says, at having punished them without soiling his hands with their blood (*ioueux de les auior puniz sans se souiller les mains en leurs sang*). They built as best they could a hut of boughs and strewed beds of leaves, until they had killed wild beasts enough to prepare their skins. Their store of hard bread lasted them but a little while, but there were fruits around them, and there was fresh water near by. "Yet it was terrible," says Thevet's old narrative, "to hear the frightful sounds which the evil spirits made around them, and how they tried to break down their abode, and showed themselves in various forms of frightful animals; yet at last, conquered by the constancy and perseverance of these repentant Christians, the tormentors afflicted or disquieted them no more, save that often in the night they heard cries so loud that it seemed as if more than five thousand men were assembled together" (*plus de cent mil hōmes qui fussent ensemble*).

So passed many months of desolation, and

alas! the husband was the first to yield. Daily he climbed the rocks to look for vessels; each night he descended sadder and sadder; he waked while the others slept. Feeling that it was he who had brought distress upon the rest, he concealed his depression, but it soon was past concealing; he only redoubled his care and watching as his wife grew the stronger of the two; and he faded slowly away and died. His wife had nothing to sustain her spirits except the approach of maternity — she would live for her child. When the child was born and baptized in the name of the Holy Church, though without the Church's full ceremonies, Marguerite felt the strength of motherhood; became a better huntress, a better provider. A new sorrow came; in the sixteenth or seventeenth month of her stay, the old nurse died also, and not long after the baby followed. Marguerite now seemed to herself deserted, even by Heaven itself; she was alone in that northern island without comradeship; her husband, child, and nurse gone; dependent for very food on the rapidly diminishing supply of ammunition. Her head swam; for months she saw visions almost constantly, which only strenuous prayer banished, and only the acquired habit of the chase enabled her, almost mechanically, to secure meat to support life. Fortunately, those especial sights and sounds of demons which had haunted her imagination during the first days and nights on the island, did not recur; but the wild beasts gathered round her the more when there was only one gun to alarm them; and she once shot three bears in a day, — one a white bear, of which she secured the skin.

What imagination can depict the terrors of those lonely days and still lonelier nights? Most persons left as solitary tenants of an island have dwelt, like Alexander Selkirk, in regions nearer the tropics, where there was at least a softened air, a fertile soil, and the Southern Cross above their heads; but to be solitary in a prolonged winter, to be alone with the Northern Lights, — this offered peculiar terrors. To be ice-bound, to hear the wolves in their long and dreary howl, to protect the very graves of her beloved from being dug up, to watch the floating icebergs, not knowing what new and savage visitor might be borne by them to the island, what a complication of terror was this for Marguerite!

For two years and five months in all she dwelt upon the Isle of Demons, the last year wholly alone. Then, as she stood upon the shore, some Breton fishing-smacks, seeking codfish, came in sight. Making signals with fire and calling for aid, she drew them nearer; but she was now dressed in furs only, and seemed to them but one of the fancied demons of the island. Beating up slowly and watchfully toward the shore, they came within hearing of her voice and she told her dreary tale. At last they took her in charge, and bore her back to France with the bearskins she had prepared; and taking refuge in the village of Nautron, in a remote province (Perigord), where she could escape the wrath of Roberval, she told her story to Thevet, the explorer, to the Princess Marguerite of Navarre (sister of Francis I.), and to others. Thevet tells it in his "Cosmographie," and Marguerite of Navarre in her "Cent Nouvelles Nouvelles."

She told Thevet that after the first two months, the demons came to her no more, until she was left wholly alone; then they renewed their visits, but not continuously, and she felt less fear. Thevet also records of her this touching confession, that when the time came for her to embark, in the Breton ship, for home, there came over her a strong impulse to refuse the embarkation, but rather to die in that solitary place, as her husband, her child, and her servant had already died. This profound touch of human nature does more than anything else to confirm the tale as substantially true. Certain it is that the lonely island which appeared so long on the old maps as the Isle of Demons (l'Isola de Demoni) appears differently in later ones as the Lady's Island (l'Isle de la Demoiselle).

The Princess Marguerite of Navarre, who died in 1549, seems also to have known her namesake at her retreat in Perigord, gives some variations from Thevet's story, and describes her as having been put on shore with her husband, because of frauds which he had practised on Roberval; nor does she speak of the nurse or of the child. But she gives a similar description of Marguerite's stay on the island, after

his death, and says, that although she lived what
might seem a bestial life as to her body, it was
a life wholly angelic as regarded her soul
(*aînsî vivant, quant au corps, de vie bestiale, et
quant à l'esprit, de vie angelicque*).  She had, the
princess also says, a mind cheerful and content;
in a body emaciated and half dead.  She was
afterwards received with great honor in France,
according to the princess, and was encouraged
to establish a school for little children, where
she taught reading and writing to the daughters
of high-born families.  " And by this honest
industry," says the princess, " she supported
herself during the remainder of her life, having
no other wish than to exhort every one to love
and confidence towards God, offering them as
an example, the great pity which he had shown
for her."

## XX

## BIMINI AND THE FOUNTAIN OF YOUTH

WHEN Juan Ponce de Leon set forth from Porto Rico, March 13, 1512, to seek the island of Bimini and its Fountain of Youth, he was moved by the love of adventure more than by that of juvenility, for he was then but about fifty, a time when a cavalier of his day thought himself but in his prime. He looked indeed with perpetual sorrow — as much of it as a Spaniard of those days could feel — upon his kinsman Luis Ponce, once a renowned warrior, but on whom age had already, at sixty-five, laid its hand in earnest. There was little in this slowly moving veteran to recall one who had shot through the lists at the tournament, and had advanced with his short sword at the bull fight, — who had ruled his vassals, and won the love of high-born women. It was a vain hope of restored youth

which had brought Don Luis from Spain to
Porto Rico four years before; and, when Ponce
de Leon had subdued that island, his older
kinsman was forever beseeching him to carry
his flag farther, and not stop till he had reached
Bimini, and sought the Fountain of Youth.

"For what end," he said, "should you stay
here longer and lord it over these miserable
natives? Let us go where we can bathe in
those enchanted waters and be young once
more. I need it, and you will need it ere long."

"How know we," said his kinsman, "that
there is any such place?"

"All know it," said Luis. "Peter Martyr
saith that there is in Bimini a continual spring
of running water of such marvellous virtue that
the water thereof, being drunk, perhaps with
some diet, maketh old men young." And he
adds that an Indian grievously oppressed with
old age, moved with the fame of that fountain,
and allured through the love of longer life, went
to an island, near unto the country of Florida, to
drink of the desired fountain, . . . and having well drunk and washed himself for many

days with the appointed remedies, by them who kept the bath, he is reported to have brought home a manly strength, and to have used all manly exercises. " Let us therefore go thither," he cried, " and be like him."

They set sail with three brigantines and found without difficulty the island of Bimini among the Lucayos (or Bahamas) islands ; but when they searched for the Fountain of Youth they were pointed farther westward to Florida, where there was said to be a river of the same magic powers, called the Jordan. Touching at many a fair island green with trees, and occupied by a gentle population till then undisturbed, it was not strange if, nearing the coast of Florida, both Juan Ponce de Leon and his more impatient cousin expected to find the Fountain of Youth.

They came at last to an inlet which led invitingly up among wooded banks and flowery valleys, and here the older knight said, " Let us disembark here and strike inland. My heart tells me that here at last will be found the Fountain of Youth." " Nonsense," said Juan, " our way lies by water."

"Then leave me here with my men," said Luis. He had brought with him five servants, mostly veterans, from his own estate in Spain.

A fierce discussion ended in Luis obtaining his wish, and being left for a fortnight of exploration; his kinsman promising to come for him again at the mouth of the river St. John. The men left on shore were themselves past middle age, and the more eager for their quest. They climbed a hill and watched the brigantines disappear in the distance; then set up a cross, which they had brought with them, and prayed before it bareheaded.

Sending the youngest of his men up to the top of a tree, Luis learned from him that they were on an island, after all, and this cheered him much, as making it more likely that they should find the Fountain of Youth. He saw that the ground was pawed up, as if in a cattle-range and that there was a path leading to huts. Taking this path, they met fifty Indian bowmen, who, whether large or not, seemed to them like giants. The Spaniards gave them beads and hawk-bells, and each received in return an arrow, as a token of friendship. The Indians promised them food in the morning, and brought fish, roots, and pure water ; and finding them chilly from the coldness of the night, carried them in their arms to their homes, first making four or five large fires on the way. At the houses there were many fires, and the Spaniards would have been wholly comfortable, had they not thought it just possible that they were to be offered as a sacrifice. Still fearing this, they left their Indian friends after a few days and traversed the country, stopping at every spring or fountain to test its quality. Alas! they all grew older and more worn in look, as time went on, and farther from the Fountain of Youth.

After a time they came upon new tribes of Indians, and as they went farther from the coast these people seemed more and more friendly. They treated the white men as if come from heaven,— brought them food, made them houses, carried every burden for them. Some had bows, and went upon the hills for deer, and brought half a dozen every night for their guests ; others killed hares and rabbits by arranging themselves in a circle and striking down the game with billets of wood as it ran from one to another through the woods. All this game was brought to the visitors to be breathed upon and blessed, and when this had to be done for several hundred people it became troublesome. The women also brought wild fruit, and would eat nothing till the guests had seen and touched it. If the visitors seemed offended, the natives were terrified, and apparently thought that they should die unless they had the favor of these wise and good men. Farther on, people did not come out into the paths to gather round them, as the first had done, but stayed meekly in their houses, sitting with their faces turned to the wall, and with their property heaped in the middle of the room. From these people the travellers received many valuable skins, and other gifts. Wherever there was a fountain, the natives readily showed it, but apparently knew nothing of any miraculous gift; yet they themselves were in such fine physical condition, and seemed so young and so active, that it was as if they had already bathed in some magic spring. They had wonderful endurance of heat and cold, and

Q

such health that, when their bodies were pierced through and through by arrows, they would recover rapidly from their wounds. These things convinced the Spaniards that, even if the Indians would not disclose the source of all their bodily freshness, it must, at any rate, lie somewhere in the neighborhood. Yet a little while, no doubt, and their visitors would reach it.

It was a strange journey for these gray and careworn men as they passed up the defiles and valleys along the St. John's River, beyond the spot where now spreads the city of Jacksonville, and even up to the woods and springs about Magnolia and Green Cove. Yellow jasmines trailed their festoons above their heads; wild roses grew at their feet; the air was filled with the aromatic odors of pine or sweet bay; the long gray moss hung from the live-oak branches; birds and butterflies of wonderful hues fluttered around them; and strange lizards crossed their paths, or looked with dull and blinking eyes from the branches. They came, at last, to one spring which widened into a natural basin, and which was so deliciously aromatic that Luis Ponce said, on emerging : " It is enough.   I have bathed in the Fountain of Youth, and henceforth I am young."   His companions tried it, and said the same : " The Fountain of Youth is found."

No time must now be lost in proclaiming the great discovery.   They obtained a boat from the natives, who wept at parting with the white strangers whom they had so loved.   In this boat they proposed to reach the mouth of the St. John, meet Juan Ponce de Leon, and carry back the news to Spain.   But one native, whose wife and children they had cured, and who had grown angry at their refusal to stay longer, went down to the water's edge and, sending an arrow from his bow, transfixed Don Luis, so that even his foretaste of the Fountain could not save him, and he died ere reaching the mouth of the river. If Don Luis ever reached what he sought, it was in another world.   But those who have ever bathed in Green Cove Spring, near Magnolia, on the St. John's River, will be ready to testify that, had he but stayed there longer, he would have found something to recall his visions of the Fountain of Youth.

# NOTES

## PREFACE

A FULL account of the rediscovery of the Canaries in 1341 will be found in Major's "Life of Prince Henry of Portugal" (London, 1868), p. 138. For the statement as to the lingering belief in the Jacquet Island, see Winsor's "Columbus," p. 111. The extract from Cowley is given by Herman Melville in his picturesque paper on "The Encantadas" (*Putnam's Magazine*, III. 319). In Harris's "Voyages" (1702) there is a map giving "Cowley's Inchanted Isl." (I. 78), but there is no explanation of the name. The passage quoted by Melville is not to be found in Cowley's "Voyage to Magellanica and Polynesia," given by Harris in the same volume, and must be taken from Cowley's "Voyage round the Globe," which I have not found in any library.

## I. ATLANTIS

FOR the original narrative of Socrates, see Plato's "Timæus" and "Critias," in each of which it is given. For further information see the chapter on the Geographical Knowledge of the Ancients by W. H. Tillinghast, in Winsor's "Narrative and Critical History of America," I. 15. He mentions (I. 19, note) a map printed at Amsterdam in 1678 by Kircher, which shows Atlantis as a large island midway between Spain and

America.   Ignatius Donnelly's "Atlantis, the Antediluvian World" (N. Y. 1882), maintains that the evidence for the former existence of such an island is irresistible, and his work has been very widely read, although it is not highly esteemed by scholars.

## II.   TALIESSIN

THE Taliessin legend in its late form cannot be traced back beyond the end of the sixteenth century, but the account of the transformation is to be found in the "Book of Taliessin," a manuscript of the thirteenth century, preserved in the Hengwt Collection at Peniarth.   The Welsh bard himself is supposed to have flourished in the sixth century.   See Alfred Nutt in "The Voyage of Bram" (London, 1897), II. 86.   The traditions may be found in Lady Charlotte Guest's translation of the "Mabinogion," 2d ed., London, 1877, p. 471.   The poems may be found in the original Welsh in Skene's "Four Ancient Books of Wales," 2 vols., Edinburgh, 1868.; and he also gives a facsimile of the manuscript.

## III.   CHILDREN OF LIR

THE lovely legend of the children of Lir or Lear forms one of those three tales of the old Irish Bards which are known traditionally in Ireland as "The Three Sorrows of Story Telling."   It has been told in verse by Aubrey de Vere ("The Foray of Queen Meave, and Other Legends," London, 1882), by John Todhunter ("Three Irish Bardic Tales," London, 1896) ; and also in prose by various writers, among whom are Professor Eugene O'Curry, whose version with the Gaelic original was published

in "Atlantis," Nos. vii. and viii. ; Gerald Griffin in " The Tales
of a Jury Room " ; and Dr. Patrick Weston Joyce in " Ancient
Celtic Romances " (London, 1879). The oldest manuscript
copy of the tale in Gaelic is one in the British Museum, made
in 1718 ; but there are more modern ones in different English
and Irish libraries, and the legend itself is of much older origin.
Professor O'Curry, the highest authority, places its date before
the year 1000. ("Lectures on the Manuscript Materials of
Irish History," p. 319.)

## IV.  USHEEN

In the original legend, Oisin or Usheen is supposed to have
told his tale to St. Patrick on his arrival in Ireland ; but as the
ancient Feni were idolaters, the hero bears but little goodwill to
the saint. The Celtic text of a late form of the legend (1749)
with a version by Brian O'Looney will be found in the transactions of the Ossianic Society for 1856 (Vol. IV. p. 227);
and still more modern and less literal renderings in P. W. Joyce's
"Ancient Celtic Romances " (London, 1879), p. 385, and
in W. B. Yeats's " Wanderings of Oisin, and Other Poems "
(London, 1889), p. 1. The last is in verse and is much the best.
St. Patrick, who takes part in it, regards Niam as "a demon
thing." See also the essays entitled " L'Elysée Transatlan-
tique," by Eugene Beauvois, in the " Revue de L'Histoire des
Religions," VII. 273 (Paris, 1885), and "L'Eden Occidental "
(same, VII. 673). As to Oisin or Usheen's identity with Os-
sian, see O'Curry's " Lectures on the Manuscript Materials for
Ancient Irish History " (Dublin, 1861), pp. 209, 300 ; John
Rhys's "Hibbert Lectures " (London, 1888), p. 551. The

latter thinks the hero identical with Taliessin, as well as with Ossian, and says that the word Ossin means "a little fawn," from "os," "cervus." (See also O'Curry, p. 304.) O'Looney represents that it was a stone which Usheen threw to show his strength, and Joyce follows this view; but another writer in the same volume of the Ossianic Society transactions (p. 233) makes it a bag of sand, and Yeats follows this version. It is also to be added that the latter in later editions changes the spelling of his hero's name from Oisin to Usheen.


## V.  BRAN

THE story of Bran and his sister Branwen may be found most fully given in Lady Charlotte Guest's translation of the "Mabinogion," ed. 1877, pp. 369, 384. She considers Harlech, whence Bran came, to be a locality on the Welsh seacoast still known by that name and called also Branwen's Tower. But Rhys, a much higher authority, thinks that Bran came really from the region of Hades, and therefore from a distant island ("Arthurian Legend," p. 250, "Hibbert Lectures," pp. 94, 269). The name of "the Blessed" came from the legend of Bran's having introduced Christianity into Ireland, as stated in one of the Welsh Triads. He was the father of Caractacus, celebrated for his resistance to the Roman conquest, and carried a prisoner to Rome. Another triad speaks of King Arthur as having dug up Bran's head, for the reason that he wished to hold England by his own strength; whence followed many disasters (Guest, p. 387).

There were many Welsh legends in regard to Branwen or Bronwen (White Bosom), and what is supposed to be her grave, with an urn containing her ashes, may still be seen at a place called "Ynys Bronwen," or "the islet of Bronwen," in Anglesea. It was discovered and visited in 1813 (Guest, p. 389).

The White Mount in which Bran's head was deposited is supposed to have been the Tower of London, described by a Welsh poet of the twelfth century as "The White Eminence of London, a place of splendid fame" (Guest, p. 392).

## VI. THE CASTLE OF THE ACTIVE DOOR

THIS legend is mainly taken from different parts of Lady Charlotte Guest's translation of the "Mabinogion," with some additions and modifications from Rhys's "Hibbert Lectures" and "The Arthurian Legend."

## VIII. MERLIN

IN later years Merlin was known mainly by a series of re-markable prophecies which were attributed to him and were often said to be fulfilled by actual events in history. Thus one of the many places where Merlin's grave was said to be was Drummelzion in Tweeddale, Scotland. On the east side of the churchyard a brook called the Pansayl falls into the Tweed, and there was this prophecy as to their union : —

"When Tweed and Pansayl join at Merlin's grave,
    Scotland and England shall one monarch have."

Sir Walter Scott tells us, in his "Border Minstrelsy," that on the day of the coronation of James VI. of Scotland the Tweed accordingly overflowed and joined the Pansayl at the prophet's grave. It was also claimed by one of the witnesses at the trial of Jeanne d'Arc, that there was a prediction by Merlin that France would be saved by a peasant girl from Lorraine. These prophesies have been often reprinted, and have been translated into different languages, and there was published in London, in 1641, "The Life of Merlin, surnamed Ambrosius, His Prophesies and Predictions interpreted, and their Truth made Good by our English Annals." Another book was also published in London, in 1683, called "Merlin revived in a Discourse of Prophesies, Predictions, and their Remarkable Accomplishments."

## VIII. LANCELOT

THE main sources of information concerning Lancelot are the "Morte d'Arthur," Newell's "King Arthur and the Table Round," and the publications of the Early English Text Society. See also Rhys's "Arthurian Legend," pp. 127, 147, etc.

## IX. THE HALF-MAN

THE symbolical legend on which this tale is founded will be found in Lady Charlotte Guest's translation of the "Mabinogion" (London, 1877), II. p. 344. It is an almost unique instance, in the imaginative literature of that period, of a direct and avowed allegory. There is often allegory, but it is usually contributed by modern interpreters, and would sometimes greatly astound the original fabulists.

## X. ARTHUR

THE earliest mention of the island of Avalon, or Avilion, in connection with the death of Arthur, is a slight one by the old English chronicler, Geoffrey of Monmouth (Book XI. c. 2), and the event is attributed by him to the year 542. Wace's French romance was an enlargement of Geoffrey ; and the narrative of Layamon (at the close of the twelfth century) an explanation of that of Wace. Layamon's account of the actual death of Arthur, as quoted in the text, is to be found in the translation, a very literal one, by Madden (Madden's " Layamon's Brut," III. pp. 140–146).

The earliest description of the island itself is by an anonymous author known as " Pseudo-Gildas," supposed to be a thirteenth-century Breton writer ( Meyer's " Voyage of Bram," I. p. 237), and quoted by Archbishop Usher in his " British Ecclesiastical Antiquities " (1637), p. 273, who thus describes it in Latin hexameters : —

" Cingitur oceano memorabilis insula nullis
  Desolata bonis : non fur, nec prædo, nec hostis
  Insidiatur ibi : nec vis, nec bruma nec æstas,
  Immoderata furit.   Pax et concordia, pubes
  Ver manent æternum.   Nec flos, nec lilia desunt,
  Nec rosa, nec violæ : flores et poma sub unâ
  Fronde gerit pomus.   Habitant sine labe cruoris
  Semper ibi juvenes cum virgine : nulla senectus,
  Nulla vis morbi, nullus dolor ; omnia plena
  Lætitiæ ; nihil hic proprium, communia quæque.
    Regit virgo locis et rebus præsidet istis,

> Virginibus stipata suis, pulcherrima pulchris ;
> Nympha decens vultu, generosis patribus orta,
> Consilio pollens, medicinæ nobilis arte.
> At simul Arthurus regni diadema reliquit,
> Substitutique sibi regem, se transtulit illic ;
> Anno quingeno quadragenoque secundo
> Post incarnatum sine patris semine natum.
> Immodicè læsus, Arthurus tendit ad aulam
> Regis Avallonis ; ubi virgo regia vulnus
> Illius tractans, sanati membra reservat
> Ipsa sibi : vivuntque simul ; si credere fas est.''

A translation of this passage into rhyming English follows ; both of these being taken from Way's '' Fabliaux '' (London, 1815), II. pp. 233–235.

> '' By the main ocean's wave encompass'd, stands
> A memorable isle, fill'd with all good :
> No thief, no spoiler there, no wily foe
> With stratagem of wasteful war ; no rage
> Of heat intemperate, or of winter's cold ;
> But spring, full blown, with peace and concord reigns :
> Prime bliss of heart and season, fitliest join'd !
> Flowers fail not there : the lily and the rose,
> With many a knot of fragrant violets bound ;
> And, loftier, clustering down the bended boughs,
> Blossom with fruit combin'd, rich apples hang.

> '' Beneath such mantling shades for ever dwell
> In virgin innocence and honour pure,
> Damsels and youths, from age and sickness free,

And ignorant of woe, and fraught with joy,
In choice community of all things best.
    O'er these, and o'er the welfare of this land,
Girt with her maidens, fairest among fair,
Reigns a bright virgin sprung from generous sires,
In counsel strong, and skill'd in med'cine's lore.
Of her (Britannia's diadem consign'd
To other brow), for his deep wound and wide
Great Arthur sought relief: hither he sped
(Nigh two and forty and five hundred years
Since came the incarnate Son to save mankind),
And in Avallon's princely hall repos'd.
His wound the royal damsel search'd; she heal'd;
And in this isle still holds him to herself
In sweet society, — so fame say true!"


## XI.  MAELDUIN

THIS narrative is taken partly from Nutt's "Voyage of
Bram" (I. 162) and partly from Joyce's "Ancient Celtic Romances." The latter, however, allows Maelduin sixty comrades instead of seventeen, which is Nutt's version. There are
copies of the original narrative in the Erse language at the
British Museum, and in the library of Trinity College, Dublin.
The voyage, which may have had some reality at its founda-
tion, is supposed to have taken place about the year 700 A.D.
It belongs to the class known as Imrama, or sea-expeditions.
Another of these is the voyage of St. Brandan, and another is
that of "the sons of O'Corra." A poetical translation of this
last has been made by T. D. Sullivan of Dublin, and published

in his volume of poems.     (Joyce, p. xiii.)     All these voyages
illustrated the wider and wider space assigned on the Atlantic
ocean to the enchanted islands until they were finally identified,
in some cases, with the continent which Columbus found.

## XII.  ST. BRANDAN

THE legend of St. Brandan, which was very well known in
the Middle Ages, was probably first written in Latin prose near
the end of the eleventh century, and is preserved in manuscript
in many English libraries.     An English metrical version, written
probably about the beginning of the fourteenth century, is printed
under the editorship of Thomas Wright in the publications of the
Percy Society, London, 1844 (XIV.), and it is followed in the
same volume by an English prose version of 1527.    A partial
narrative in Latin prose, with an English version, may be found
in W. J. Rees's " Lives of the Cambro-British Saints " (Llan-
dovery, 1853), pp. 251, 575.    The account of Brandan in the
Acta Sanctorum of the Bollandists may be found under May 16,
the work being arranged under saints' days.    This account ex-
cludes the more legendary elements.    The best sketch of the
supposed island appears in the *Nouvelles Annales des Voyages* for
1845 (p. 293), by D'Avezac.    Professor O'Curry places the
date of the alleged voyage or voyages at about the year 560 (" Lectures on the Manuscript Materials for Irish History," p. 289).
Good accounts of the life in the great monasteries of Brandan's
period may be found in Digby's " Mores Catholici " or "Ages
of Faith " ; in Montalembert's " Monks of the West " (translation) ; in Villemarqué's " La Legende Celtique et la Poésie
des Cloistres en Irlande, en Cambrie et en Bretagne " (Paris,

1864). The poem on St. Brandan, stanzas from which are quoted in the text, is by Denis Florence McCarthy, and may be found in the *Dublin University Magazine* (XXXI. p. 89); and there is another poem on the subject — a very foolish burlesque — in the same magazine (LXXXIX. p. 471). Matthew Arnold's poem with the same title appeared in *Fraser's Magazine* (LXII. p. 133), and may be found in the author's collected works in the form quoted below.

The legends of St. Brandan, it will be observed, resemble so much the tales of Sindbad the Sailor and others in the "Arabian Nights" — which have also the island-whale, the singing birds, and other features — that it is impossible to doubt that some features of tradition were held in common with the Arabs of Spain.

In later years (the twelfth century), a geographer named Honoré d'Autun declared, in his "Image of the World," that there was in the ocean a certain island agreeable and fertile beyond all others, now unknown to men, once discovered by chance and then lost again, and that this island was the one which Brandan had visited. In several early maps, before the time of Columbus, the Madeira Islands appear as "The Fortunate Islands of St. Brandan," and on the famous globe of Martin Behaim, made in the very year when Columbus sailed, there is a large island much farther west than Madeira, and near the equator, with an inscription saying that in the year 565, St. Brandan arrived at this island and saw many wondrous things, returning to his own land afterwards. Columbus heard this island mentioned at Ferro, where men declared that they had seen it in the distance. Later, the chart of Ortelius, in the sixteenth century, carried it to the neighborhood of Ireland;

then it was carried south again, and was supposed all the time to change its place through enchantment, and when Emanuel of Portugal, in 1519, renounced all claim to it, he described it as "The Hidden Island." In 1570 a Portuguese expedition was sent which claimed actually to have touched the mysterious island, indeed to have found there the vast impression of a human foot — doubtless of the baptized giant Mildus — and also a cross nailed to a tree, and three stones laid in a triangle for cooking food. Departing hastily from the island, they left two sailors behind, but could never find the place again.

Again and again expeditions were sent out in search of St. Brandan's island, usually from the Canaries — one in 1604 by Acosta, one in 1721 by Dominguez; and several sketches of the island, as seen from a distance, were published in 1759 by a Franciscan priest in the Canary Islands, named Viere y Clarijo, including one made by himself on May 3, 1759, about 6 A.M., in presence of more than forty witnesses. All these sketches depict the island as having its chief length from north to south, and formed of two unequal hills, the highest of these being at the north, they having between them a depression covered with trees. The fact that this resembles the general form of Palma, one of the Canary Islands, has led to the belief that it may have been an ocean mirage, reproducing the image of that island, just as the legends themselves reproduce, here and there, the traditions of the "Arabian Nights."

In a map drawn by the Florentine physician, Toscanelli, which was sent by him to Columbus in 1474 to give his impression of the Asiatic coast, — lying, as he supposed, across the Atlantic, — there appears the island of St. Brandan. It is as large as all the Azores or Canary Islands or Cape de Verde Islands put together; its southern tip just touches the equator, and it lies about half-way between the Cape de Verde Islands and Zipangu or Japan, which was then believed to lie on the other side of the Atlantic. Mr. Winsor also tells us that the apparition of this island "sometimes came to sailors' eyes" as late as the last century (Winsor's "Columbus," 112).

He also gives a reproduction of Toscanelli's map now lost, as far as can be inferred from descriptions (Winsor, p. 110).

The following is Matthew Arnold's poem: —

### SAINT BRANDAN

Saint Brandan sails the northern main;
The brotherhoods of saints are glad.
He greets them once, he sails again;
So late! — such storms! — the Saint is mad!

He heard, across the howling seas,
Chime convent-bells on wintry nights;
He saw, on spray-swept Hebrides,
Twinkle the monastery lights;

But north, still north, Saint Brandan steer'd —
And now no bells, no convents more!
The hurtling Polar lights are near'd,
The sea without a human shore.

At last — (it was the Christmas-night;
Stars shone after a day of storm) —
He sees float past an iceberg white,
And on it — Christ! — a living form.

R

That furtive mien, that scowling eye,
Of hair that red and tufted fell —
It is — oh, where shall Brandan fly ? —
The traitor Judas, out of hell !

Palsied with terror, Brandan sate ;
The moon was bright, the iceberg near.
He hears a voice sigh humbly : " Wait !
By high permission I am here.

" One moment wait, thou holy man !
On earth my crime, my death, they knew ;
My name is under all men's ban —
Ah, tell them of my respite, too !

" Tell them, one blessed Christmas-night —
(It was the first after I came,
Breathing self-murder, frenzy, spite,
To rue my guilt in endless flame) —

" I felt, as I in torment lay
'Mid the souls plagued by heavenly power,
An angel touch my arm and say :
*Go hence, and cool thyself an hour !*

" ' Ah, whence this mercy, Lord ? ' I said ;
*The Leper recollect,* said he,
*Who ask'd the passers-by for aid,*
*In Joppa, and thy charity.*

" Then I remember'd how I went,
  In Joppa, through the public street,
  One morn when the sirocco spent
  Its storm of dust with burning heat ;

" And in the street a leper sate,
  Shivering with fever, naked, old ;
  Sand raked his sores from heel to pate,
  The hot wind fever'd him five-fold.

" He gazed upon me as I pass'd,
  And murmur'd : *Help me, or I die !* —
  To the poor wretch my cloak I cast,
  Saw him look eased, and hurried by.

" Oh, Brandan, think what grace divine,
  What blessing must full goodness shower,
  When fragment of it small, like mine,
  Hath such inestimable power !

" Well-fed, well-clothed, well-friended, I
  Did that chance act of good, that one !
  Then went my way to kill and lie —
  Forgot my good as soon as done.

" That germ of kindness, in the womb
  Of mercy caught, did not expire ;
  Outlives my guilt, outlives my doom,
  And friends me in this pit of fire.

" Once every year, when carols wake
  On earth the Christmas-night's repose,
  Arising from the sinner's lake,
  I journey to these healing snows.

" I stanch with ice my burning breast,
  With silence balm my whirling brain ;
  O Brandan ! to this hour of rest
  That Joppan leper's ease was pain.''

  Tears started to Saint Brandan's eyes ;
  He bow'd his head, he breathed a prayer —
  Then look'd, and lo, the frosty skies !
  The iceberg, and no Judas there !

The island of St. Brandan's was sometimes supposed to lie in the Northern Atlantic, sometimes farther south. It often appears as the Fortunate Isle or Islands, " Insulæ Fortunatæ '' or " Beatæ.''

On some early maps (1306 to 1471) there is an inlet on the western coast of Ireland called " Lacus Fortunatus,'' which is filled with Fortunate Islands to the number of 358 (Humboldt, "Examen," II. p. 159), and in one map of 1471 both these and the supposed St. Brandan's group appear in different parts of the ocean under the same name. When the Canary Islands were discovered, they were supposed to be identical with St. Brandan's, but the latter was afterwards supposed to lie southeast of them. After the discovery of the Azores various expeditions were sent to search for St. Brandan's until about 1721. It was last reported as seen in 1759. A full bibliography will be found in Winsor's "Narrative and Critical History," I. p. 48, and also in Humboldt's "Examen," II. p. 163, and early maps containing St. Brandan's will be found in Winsor (I. pp. 54, 58). The first of these is Pizigani's (1387), containing "Ysolæ dictæ Fortunatæ," and the other that of Ortelius (1587), containing "S. Brandain."

## XIII.  HY–BRASAIL

"THE people of Aran, with characteristic enthusiasm, fancy, that at certain periods, they see *Hy-Brasail*, elevated far to the west in their watery horizon. This has been the universal tradition of the ancient Irish, who supposed that a great part of Ireland had been swallowed by the sea, and that the sunken part often rose and was seen hanging in the horizon : such was the popular notion. The Hy-Brasail of the Irish is evidently a part of the Atlantis of Plato; who, in his 'Timæus,' says that that island was totally swallowed up by a prodigious earthquake." (O'Flaherty's "Discourse on the History and Antiquities of the Southern Islands of Aran, lying off the West Coast of Ireland," 1824, p. 139.)

The name appeared first (1351) on the chart called the Medicean Portulana, applied to an island off the Azores. In Pizigani's map (1367) there appear three islands of this name, two off the Azores and one off Ireland. From this time the name appears constantly in maps, and in 1480 a man named John Jay went out to discover the island on July 14, and returned unsuccessful on September 18. He called it Barsyle or Brasylle ; and Pedro d'Ayalo, the Spanish Ambassador, says that such voyages were made for seven years "according to the fancies of the Genoese, meaning Sebastian Cabot." Humboldt thinks that the wood called Brazil-wood was supposed to have come from it, as it was known before the South American Brazil was discovered.

A manuscript history of Ireland, written about 1636, in the Library of the Royal Irish Academy, says that Hy-Brasail was discovered by a Captain Rich, who saw its harbor but could never reach it. It is mentioned by Jeremy Taylor ("Dissuasives from Popery," 1667), and the present narrative is founded partly on an imaginary one, printed in a pamphlet in London, 1675, and reprinted in Hardiman's "Irish Minstrelsy" (1831), II. p. 369. The French Geographer Royal, M. Tassin, thinks that the island may have been identical with Porcupine Bank, once above water. In Jeffrey's atlas (1776) it appears as "the imaginary island of O'Brasil." "Brazil Rock" appears on a chart of Purdy, 1834 (Humboldt's "Examen Critique," II. p. 163). Two rocks always associated with it, Mayda and Green Rock, appear on an atlas issued in 1866. See bibliography in Winsor's "Narrative and Critical History," I. p. 49, where there are a number of maps depicting it (I. pp. 54–57). The name of the island is derived by Celtic scholars from *breas*, large, and *i*, island; or, according to O'Brien's "Irish Dictionary," its other form of O'Brasile means a large imaginary island (Hardiman's "Irish Minstrelsy," I. p. 369). There are several families named Brazil in County Waterford, Ireland ("Transactions of the Ossianic Society, Dublin," 1854, I. p. 81). The following poem about the island, by Gerald Griffin, will be found in Sparling's "Irish Minstrelsy" (1888), p. 427 :—

### Hy-Brasail, the Isle of the Blest

On the ocean that hollows the rocks where ye dwell
A shadowy land has appeared, as they tell ;
Men thought it a region of sunshine and rest,
And they called it Hy-Brasail, the isle of the blest.
From year unto year on the ocean's blue rim,
The beautiful spectre showed lovely and dim ;
The golden clouds curtained the deep where it lay,
And it looked like an Eden away, far away !


A peasant who heard of the wonderful tale,
In the breeze of the Orient loosened his sail ;
From Ara, the holy, he turned to the west,
For though Ara was holy, Hy-Brasail was blest.
He heard not the voices that called from the shore —
He heard not the rising wind's menacing roar ;
Home, kindred, and safety he left on that day,
And he sped to Hy-Brasail, away, far away !


Morn rose on the deep, and that shadowy isle,
O'er the faint rim of distance, reflected its smile ;
Noon burned on the wave, and that shadowy shore
Seemed lovelily distant, and faint as before ;
Lone evening came down on the wanderer's track,
And to Ara again he looked timidly back ;
O far on the verge of the ocean it lay,
Yet the isle of the blest was away, far away !

Rash dreamer, return ! O ye winds of the main,
Bear him back to his own peaceful Ara again,
Rash fool ! for a vision of fanciful bliss,
To barter thy calm life of labor and peace.
The warning of reason was spoken in vain ;
He never revisited Ara again !
Night fell on the deep, amidst tempest and spray,
And he died on the waters, away, far away !

## XIV.  ISLAND OF SATAN'S HAND

THE early part of this narrative is founded on Professor
O'Curry's Lectures on the manuscript materials of Irish history ;
it being another of those "Imrama" or narratives of ocean
expeditions to which the tale of St. Brandan belongs.  The
original narrative lands the three brothers ultimately in Spain,
and it is a curious fact that most of what we know of the island
of Satanaxio or Satanajio — which remained so long on the
maps — is taken from an Italian narrative of three other brothers,
cited by Formaleoni, "Il Pellegrinaccio di tre giovanni," by
Christoforo Armeno (Gaffarel, "Les Iles Fantastiques," p. 91).
The coincidence is so peculiar that it offered an irresistible
temptation to link the two trios of brothers into one narrative
and let the original voyagers do the work of exploration.
The explanation given by Gaffarel to the tale is the same that
I have suggested as possible.  He says in "Iles Fantastiques de
l'Atlantique" (p. 12), "S'il nous était permis d'aventurer une
hypothèse, nous croirions voluntiers que les navigateurs de
l'époque rencontrèrent, en s'aventurant dans l'Atlantique,
quelques-uns de ces gigantesques icebergs, ou montagnes de

glace, arrachés aux banquises du pôle nord, et entrainés au sud par les courants, dont la rencontre, assez fréquente, est, même aujourd'hui, tellement redoutée par les capitaines. Ces icebergs, quand ils se heurtent contre un navire, le coulent à pic ; et comme ils arrivent à l'improviste, escortés par d'épais brouillards, ils paraissent réellement sortir du sein des flots, comme sortait la main de Satan, pour precipiter au fond de l'abîme matelots et navires." As to the name itself there has been much discussion. On the map of Bianco (1436) — reproduced in Winsor, I. p. 54 — the name "Ya de Laman-satanaxio" distinctly appears, and this was translated by both Formaleoni and Humboldt as meaning "the Island of the Hand of Satan." D'Avezac was the first to suggest that the reference was to two separate islands, the one named "De la Man" or "Danman," and the other "Satanaxio." He further suggests — followed by Gaffarel — that the name of the island may originally have been San Atanagio, thus making its baptism a tribute to St. Athanasius instead of to Satan. This would certainly have been a curious transformation, and almost as unexpected in its way as the original conversion of the sinful brothers from outlaws to missionaries.

## XV.  ANTILLIA

THE name Antillia appears first, but not very clearly, on the Pizigani map of 1367 ; then clearly on a map of 1424, preserved at Weimar, on that of Bianco in 1436, and on the globe of Beheim in 1492, which adds in an inscription the story of the Seven Bishops. On some maps of the sixteenth and seventeenth centuries there appears near it a smaller island under the name of Sette Cidade, or Sete Ciudades, which is properly another name for the same island. Toscanelli, in his famous letter to Columbus, recommended Antillia as a good way-station for his voyage to India. The island is said by tradition to have been re-discovered by a Portuguese sailor in 1447. Tradition says that this sailor went hastily to the court of Portugal to announce the discovery, but was blamed for not having remained longer, and so fled. It was supposed to be "a large, rectangular island extending from north to south, lying in the mid Atlantic about lat. 35 N." An ample bibliography will be found in Winsor's "Narrative and Critical History," I. p. 48, with maps containing Antillia, I. pp. 54 (Pizigani's), 56, 58.

After the discovery of America, Peter Martyr states (in 1493) that Hispaniola and the adjacent islands were " Antillæ insulæ," meaning that they were identical with the group surrounding the fabled Antillia (Winsor's " Narrative and Critical History," I. p. 49) ; and Schöner, in the dedicatory letter of his globe of 1523, says that the king of Castile, through Columbus, has discovered *Antiglias Hispaniam Cubam quoque*. It was thus that the name Antilles came to be applied to the islands discovered by Columbus; just as the name Brazil was transferred from an imaginary island to the new continent, and the name Seven Cities was applied to the pueblos of New Mexico by those who discovered them. (See J. H. Simpson, " Coronado's March in Search of the Seven Cities of Cibola," Smithsonian Institution, 1869, pp. 209–340.)

The sailor who re-discovered them said that the chief desire of the people was to know whether the Moors still held Spain (Gaffarel, " Iles Fantastiques," p. 3). In a copy of " Ptolemy " addressed to Pope Urban VI. about 1380, before the alleged visit of the Portuguese, it was stated of the people at Antillia that they lived in a Christian manner, and were most prosperous, " Hic populus christianissime vivit, omnibus divitiis seculi hujus plenus " (D'Avezac, " Nouvelles Annales des voyages," 1845, II. p. 55).

It was afterwards held by some that the island of Antillia was identical with St. Michael in the Azores, where a certain cluster of stone huts still bears the name of Seven Cities, and the same name is associated with a small lake by which they stand. (Humboldt's " Examen Critique," Paris, 1837, II. p. 203 ; Gaffarel, " Iles Fantastiques," p. 3.)

## XVI. HARALD THE VIKING

THE tales of the Norse explorations of America are now accessible in many forms, the most convenient of these being in the edition of E. L. Slafter, published by the Prince Society. As to the habits of the Vikings, the most accessible authorities are " The Age of the Vikings," by Du Chaillu, and " The Sea Kings of Norway," by Laing. The writings of the late Professor E. N. Horsford are well known, but his opinions are not yet generally accepted by students. His last work, " Leif's House in Vineland," with his daughter's supplementary essay on " Graves of the Northmen," is probably the most interesting of the series (Boston, 1893). In Longfellow's " Saga of King Olaf " (II.), included in " Tales of a Wayside Inn," there is a description of the athletic sports practised by the Vikings, which are moreover described with the greatest minuteness by Du Chaillu.

## XVII.  NORUMBEGA

THE narrative of Champlain's effort to find Norumbega in
1632 may be found in Otis's "Voyages of Champlain" (II.
p. 38), and there is another version in the *Magazine of American History* (I. p. 321).   The whole legend of the city is
well analyzed in the same magazine (I. p. 14) by Dr. De
Costa under the title "The Lost City of New England."   In
another volume he recurs to the subject (IX. p. 168), and
gives (IX. p. 200) a printed copy of David Ingram's narrative,
from the original in the Bodleian Library.   He also discusses
the subject in Winsor's "Narrative and Critical History" (IV.
p. 77, etc.), where he points out that "the insular character of
the Norumbega region is not purely imaginary, but is based on
the fact that the Penobscot region affords a continued water-
course to the St. Lawrence, which was travelled by the Maine
Indians."   Ramusio's map of 1559 represents "Nurumbega"
as a large island, well defined (Winsor, IV. p. 91); and so
does that of Ruscelli (Winsor, IV. p. 92), the latter spelling it
"Nurumberg."   Some geographers supposed it to extend as far
as Florida.   The name was also given to a river (probably the
Penobscot) and to a cape.   The following is Longfellow's
poem on the voyage of Sir Humphrey Gilbert : —


### SIR HUMPHREY GILBERT

Southward with fleet of ice
  Sailed the corsair Death ;
Wild and fast blew the blast,
  And the east-wind was his breath.

His lordly ships of ice
  Glisten in the sun ;
On each side, like pennons wide,
  Flashing crystal streamlets run.

His sails of white sea-mist
  Dripped with silver rain ;
But where he passed there were cast
  Leaden shadows o'er the main.

Eastward from Campobello
  Sir Humphrey Gilbert sailed ;
Three days or more seaward he bore,
  Then, alas ! the land-wind failed.

Alas ! the land-wind failed,
  And ice-cold grew the night ;
And nevermore, on sea or shore,
  Should Sir Humphrey see the light.

He sat upon the deck,
  The Book was in his hand ;
"Do not fear !  Heaven is as near,"
  He said, "by water as by land !"

In the first watch of the night,
  Without a signal's sound,
Out of the sea, mysteriously,
  The fleet of Death rose all around.

The moon and the evening star
  Were hanging in the shrouds ;
Every mast, as it passed,
  Seemed to rake the passing clouds.


They grappled with their prize,
  At midnight black and cold !
As of a rock was the shock ;
  Heavily the ground-swell rolled.


Southward through day and dark,
  They drift in close embrace,
With mist and rain, o'er the open main ;
  Yet there seems no change of place.


Southward, forever southward,
  They drift through dark and day ;
And like a dream, in the Gulf-Stream
  Sinking, vanish all away.


## XVIII.  GUARDIANS OF THE ST. LAWRENCE

FOR authorities for this tale see "Voyages of Samuel de Champlain," translated by Charles Pomeroy Otis, Ph.D., with memoir by the Rev. E. F. Slafter, A.M., Boston, 1880 (I. pp. 116, 289, II. p. 52). The incident of the disguised Indians occurred, however, to the earlier explorer, Jacques Cartier. (See my "Larger History of the United States," p. 112.)

## XIX.  ISLAND OF DEMONS

THE tale of the Isle of Demons is founded on a story told
first by Marguerite of Navarre in her "Heptameron" (LXVII.
Nouvelle), and then with much variation and amplification by
the very untrustworthy traveller Thevet in his "Cosmographie"
(1571), Livre XXIII. c. vi.  The only copy of the latter work
known to me is in the Carter-Brown Library at Providence,
R.I., and the passage has been transcribed for me through the
kindness of A. E. Winship, Esq., librarian, who has also
sent me a photograph of a woodcut representing the lonely
woman shooting at a bear.  A briefer abstract of the story
is in Winsor's "Narrative and Critical History" (IV. p. 66,
note), but it states, perhaps erroneously, that Thevet knew
Marguerite only through the Princess of Navarre, whereas that
author claims — though his claim is never worth much — that
he had the story from the poor woman herself, "*La pauvre
femme estant arriuvee en France . . . et venue en la ville de
Nautron, pays de Perigort lors que i'y estois, me feit le discours
de toutes ses fortunes passées.*"

The Island of Demons appears on many old maps which may be
found engraved in Winsor, IV. pp. 91, 92, 93, 100, 373, etc. ;
also as "Isla de demonios" in Sebastian Cabot's map (1544)
reprinted in Dr. S. E. Dawson's valuable "Voyages of the
Cabots," in the Transactions of the Royal Society of Canada
for 1897.  He also gives Ruysch's map (1508), in which a
cluster of islands appears in the same place, marked "Insulæ
dæmonum."  Harrisse, in his "Notes sur la Nouvelle France"
(p. 278), describes the three sufferers as having been abandoned

by Roberval *à trente six lieues des côtes de Canada, dans une isle deserte qui fut depuis désignée sous le nom de l'Isle de la Demoiselle, pres de l'embouchure de la Rivière St. Paul ou des Saumons.* I have not, however, been able to identify this island. Parkman also says ("Pioneers of France," p. 205) that Roberval's pilot, in his *routier,* or logbook, speaks often of "Les Isles de la Demoiselle," evidently referring to Marguerite. The brief account by the Princess of Navarre follows:—

## LXVII<sup>e</sup> Nouvelle

Une pauvre femme, pour sauver la vie de son mary, hasarda la sienne, et ne l'abandonna jusqu'à la mort.

C'est que faisant le dict Robertval un voiage sur la mer, duquel il estoit chef par le commandement du Roy son maistre, en l'isle de Canadas; auquel lieu avoit délibéré, si l'air du païs euste esté commode, de demourer et faire villes et chasteaulx; en quoy il fit tel commencement, que chacun peut sçavoir. Et, pour habituer le pays de Chrestiens, mena avecq luy de toutes sortes d'artisans, entre lesquelz y avoit un homme, qui fut si malheureux, qu'il trahit son maistre et le mist en dangier d'estre prins des gens du pays. Mais Dieu voulut que son entreprinse fut si tost congneue, qu'elle ne peut nuyre au cappitaine Robertval, lequel feit prendre ce meschant traistre, le voulant pugnir comme il l'avoit mérité; ce qui eust esté faict, sans sa femme qui avoit suivy son mary par les périlz de la mer; et ne le voulut abandonner à la mort, mais avecq force larmes feit tant, avecq le cappitaine et toute la compaignye, que, tant pour la pitié d'icelle que pour le service qu'elle leur avoit faict, luy accorda sa requeste qui fut telle, que le mary et la femme furent

laissez en une petite isle, sur la mer, où il n'habitoit que bestes
saulvaiges ; et leur fut permis de porter avecq eulx ce dont ilz
avoient nécessité. Les pauvres gens, se trouvans tous seulz en
la compaignye des bestes saulvaiges et cruelles, n'eurent recours
que à Dieu seul, qui avoit esté toujours le ferme espoir de ceste
pauvre femme. Et, comme celle qui avoit toute consolation en
Dieu, porta pour sa saulve garde, nourriture et consolation le
Nouveau Testament, lequel elle lisoit incessamment. Et, au
demourant, avecq son mary, mettoit peine d'accoustrer un petit
logis le mieulx qui'l leur estoit possible ; et, quand les lyons
et aultres bestes en aprochoient pour les dévorer, le mary avecq
sa harquebuze, et elle, avecq les pierres, se défendoient si bien,
que, non suellement les bestes ne les osoient approcher, mais
bien souvent en tuèrent de très-bonnes à manger ; ainsy, avecq
telles chairs et les herbes du païs, vesquirent quelque temps,
quand le pain leur fut failly. A la longue, le mary ne peut
porter telle nourriture ; et, à cause des eaues qu'ilz buvoient,
devint si enflé, que en peu de temps il mourut, n'aiant service
ne consolation que sa femme, laquelle le servoit de médecin et
de confesseur ; en sorte qu'il passa joieusement de ce désert en
la céleste patrie. Et la pauvre femme, demourée seulle, l'en-
terra le plus profond en terre qu'il fut possible ; si est-ce que
les bestes en eurent incontinent le sentyment, qui vindrent pour
manger la charogne. Mais la pauvre femme, en sa petite
maisonnette, de coups de harquebuze défendoit que la chair de
son mary n'eust tel sépulchre. Ainsy vivant, quant au corps,
de vie bestiale, et quant à l'esperit, de vie angélicque, passoit son
temps en lectures, contemplations, prières et oraisons ayant un
esperit joieux et content, dedans un corps emmaigry et demy mort.
Mais Celluy qui n'abandonne jamais les siens, et qui, au déses-

s

poir des autres, monstre sa puissance, ne permist que la vertu
qu'il avoit myse en ceste femme fust ignorée des hommes, mais
voulut qu'elle fust congneue à sa gloire ; et fiet que, au bout de
quelque temps, un des navires de ceste armée passant devant
ceste isle, les gens qui estoient dedans advisèrent, quelque fumée
qui leur feit souvenir de ceulx qui y avoient esté laissez, et
délibérèrent d'aller veoir ce que Dieu en avoit faict.   La pauvre
femme, voiant approcher el navire, se tira au bort de la mer,
auquel lieu la trouvèrent à leur arrivée.   Et, après en avoir
rendu louange à Dieu, les mena en sa pauvre maisonnette, et
leur monstra de quoy elle vivoit durant sa demeure ; ce que leur
eust esté incroiable, sans la congnoissance qu'ilz avoient que
Dieu est puissant de nourrir en un désert ses serviteurs, comme
au plus grandz festins du monde.   Et, ne pouvant demeurer en
tel lieu, emmenèrent la pauvre femme avecq eulx droict à la
Rochelle, où, après un navigage, ilz arrivèrent.   Et quand ilz
eurent faict entendre aux habitans la fidélité et persévérance de
ceste femme, elle fut receue à grand honneur de toutes les
Dames, qui voluntiers luy baillèrent leurs filles pour aprendre à
lire et à escripre.   Et, à cest honneste mestier-là, gaigna le
surplus de sa vie, n'aiant autre désir que d'exhorter un chaucun
à l'amour et confiance de Nostre Seigneur, se proposant pour
exemple la grande miséricorde dont il avoit usé envers elle.


## XX.  BIMINI

PARKMAN says expressly that "Ponce de Leon found the
Island of Bimini," but it is generally mentioned as having been
imaginary, and is not clearly identified among the three thousand
islands and rocks of the Bahamas.   Peter Martyr placed the

Fountain of Youth in Florida, which he may have easily supposed to be an island. Some of the features of my description are taken from the strange voyage of Cabeza da Vaca, which may be read in Buckingham Smith's translation of his narrative (Washington, D.C., 1851), or in a more condensed form in Henry Kingsley's "Tales of Old Travel," or in my own "Book of American Explorers" (N.Y., Longmans, 1894).

# NEWCASTLE ARCANA

**W-001-1**
**$3.45**
RITUAL MAGIC, by E. M. Butler.
Professor Butler traces the development of ritual magic from Akkadian inscriptions through Homer, Aeschylus, and Virgil to the Greek magical papyri, and thence with Jewish accretions to the Clavicles of the Middle Ages, and the Grimoires of the Renaissance and the Reformation. Originally published by Cambridge University Press.

**P-003-8**
**$3.95**
MAGIC WHITE AND BLACK, by Franz Hartman.
Hartmann's work is the classic treatment of theosophy and spiritual law in the natural world. Among others, he covers such topics as: the elixir of life, the philosopher's stone, hatha yoga, Rosicrucians, amulets, the astral light, Faust, Nirmanakayas, kama loca, astral projection, the mumia, and necromancy.

**T-007-0**
**$3.95**
FORTUNE TELLING FOR FUN, by Paul Showers.
Predicting the future is one of the oldest pastimes in the world. Showers discusses tea leaves, handwriting, dominoes, names, numbers, magic tables, lucky charms, ouija boards, crystal balls, fire, and moles as various means of looking into tomorrow's misty depths.

**P-008-9**
**$3.75**
THE DEVIL IN BRITAIN AND AMERICA, by John Ashton.
By far the best book ever written on Satanism, Ashton's superb study of witchcraft and demonology is now available in paperback for the first time. An illustrated compendium of case histories, dialogues, poetry, and other writings dealing with the Devil and his minions.

**P-010-0**
**$2.95**
THE BOOK OF DREAMS AND GHOSTS, by Andrew Lang.
In more than eighty separate accounts, Lang proves biographer for the Assyrian ghost, the naked ghost, the ghost that bit, the thumbless hand, the scar in the moustache, the rattlesnake ghost, and dozens of other chilling apparitions from the long-dead past. Lang wrote the well-known fantasy novel THE WORLD'S DESIRE with H. Rider Haggard.

**P-012-7**
**$2.95**
NUMEROLOGY MADE PLAIN, by Ariel Yvon Taylor.
Like astrology, numerology is a means of discovering hidden character traits, forecasting the future, and understanding the strange ways of destiny as they affect each personality. This respected volume shows the reader how to compute the number value of surnames, and provides an alphabetical listing of 1500 common given names with their numerical equivalents.

**P-019-4**
**$4.95**
THE PRACTICE OF PALMISTRY, by Comte C. de Saint-Germain.
Saint-Germain returns to the Newcastle line with his classic text on chiromancy. An incredibly detailed practical manual, this volume includes over 1000 drawings, showing each possible reading of every configuration of the hand. Two volumes in one.

**G-020-8**
**$2.95**
THOUGHT VIBRATIONS, by A. Victor Segno.
Power over one's life, and the power to control the destinies of others, depends entirely on one's mental abilities. There are men who will always be weak, because they lack the willpower to take control of their destinies. Segno clearly demonstrates the fact that thought is power, and discusses magnetism, hypnotism, and telepathy.

**P-023-2**
**$3.45**
LOST ATLANTIS, by James Bramwell.
Bramwell examines the writings of Plato, Ignatius Donnelly, and Lewis Spence, and sets forth the chief modern theories relating to the great lost continent of Atlantis. With the renewal of interest in Atlantis by modern archeologists and other researchers, Bramwell's book emerges as a clear, unprejudiced look at this ever-fascinating mystery.

**P-025-9**
**$4.95**
THIRTY YEARS AMONG THE DEAD, by Carl A. Wickland.
Dr. Wickland presents a synthesis of three decades of painstaking research into the problem of life after death, recording verbatim numerous instances of spirit communication, and discussing such unusual topics as magnetic auras, spirits and crime, drugs and ghosts, suicide, the astral planes, Christian Science, and theosophy. A classic of spiritualism.

**P-027-5**
**$4.95**
THE KABALA OF NUMBERS, by Sepharial.
A clear and original revelation of the kabalistic, or esoteric, doctrine of numerals, THE KABALA OF NUMBERS discusses the relationship between numerology and astrology, and the amazing laws which govern the occult world. This profusely illustrated manual is published for the first time as one book, including both volumes of the original text.

**P-029-1**
**$2.95**
SECRETS OF STAGE HYPNOTISM, by Professor Leonidas.
Leonidas examines the phenomenon of hypnotism, and shows how it has been used to manipulate audiences during sideshow presentations. From the very beginnings of mesmerism, to the more recent development of mind-reading and clairvoyance, Leonidas details exactly how it's done, and how to avoid getting hurt in the process. Illustrated with photographs.

**P-033-X**
**$4.95**
YOUR PSYCHIC POWERS AND HOW TO DEVELOP THEM, by Hereward Carrington.
A classic of spiritualism, Carrington's book speaks directly to today's renewed interest in things occult, providing practical instructions for developing the incredible powers latent within each persona. The discussion includes: telepathy, dreams, automatic writing, crystal gazing, prophecy, the human aura, reincarnation, astral projection, and many others.

**P-037-2**
**$4.95**
THE HISTORY AND POWER OF MIND, by Richard Ingalese.
Ingalese examines meditation, creation, the art of self-control, the cause and cure of disease, the law of opulence, thought vibration, occultism, the divine mind, and many other manifestations of the occult forces of nature.

**P-041-0**
**$3.95**
KEYS TO THE OCCULT: TWO GUIDES TO HIDDEN WISDOM, by Hereward Carrington and Willis F. Whitehead.
For the first time in a single volume, here are two works of inestimable value to the serious student of the occult. Carrington, author of YOUR PSYCHIC POWERS AND HOW TO DEVELOP THEM, examines the question of automatic writing, how to work with a ouija board, the meanings of dreams, crystal gazing, clairvoyance, telepathy, and other psychic powers. Whitehead's book, first published in 1899, discusses the Zodiac, the Tarot, the mystic powers of numbers, how to make the use a magic mirror, and others.

## VICTOR H. LINDLAHR HEALTH BOOKS

_____ H-004-6 **YOU ARE WHAT YOU EAT.**
$2.95 Lindlahr's classic revelation of diet and nutrition tells how to balance one's meals, where to find vitamins and minerals in natural foods, how to prepare dishes without destroying nutritional content, and much more. Includes complete nutritional tables for all fruits and vegetables.

_____ D-011-9 **THE LINDLAHR VITAMIN COOKBOOK.**
$2.95 Fresh foods contain all the vitamins and nutrients needed for the human body. The key to preserving these essential constituents lies in the proper preparation of meals and dishes. Complete with vitamin balance charts and recipes.

_____ H-015-1 **EAT AND REDUCE!**
$2.95 Diet the Lindlahr way, as America's leading nutritionist outlines a safe and healthy method of getting rid of extra pounds without endangering one's health. Includes diet plans and calorie tables.

_____ H-017-8 **THE NATURAL WAY TO HEALTH.**
$2.95 Here is Dr. Lindlahr's own story of his research into the natural values of organically grown foods. The secret of good health lies in living a balanced and sane life, and eating natural foods. Lindlahr anticipated much of today's findings in food research.

_____ H-040-2 **VICTOR LINDLAHR'S 7-DAY REDUCING DIET.**
$2.95 The author of YOU ARE WHAT YOU EAT presents a practical, down-to-earth reducing plan that will get the reader's weight down to where it should be—and keep it that way. Here are 201 tasty and imaginative recipes, plus a helpful question-and-answer section, calorie counters, and many important food facts.

## OTHER HEALTH BOOKS

_____ H-016-X **ROMANY REMEDIES AND RECIPES,**
$2.25 by Gipsy Petulengro.
Petulengro's book is a classic compilation of Gypsy health foods and herbal medicines, painstakingly uncovered by trial-and-error over many centuries of wandering the countrysides of Europe and America. Profusely illustrated.

_____ H-021-6 **VIEWPOINT ON NUTRITION,** by Arnold Pike.
$2.95 Dr. Pike provides nutritional highlights from his television show, including interviews with Gaylord Hauser, Linus Pauling, Eddie Albert, Julie Harris, and many others. An original Newcastle publication.

## NEWCASTLE SELF-ENRICHMENT BOOKS

_____ S-000-3 **FORTUNATE STRANGERS,**
$2.95 by Cornelius Beukenkamp, Jr.
Dr. Beukenkamp's work is a pioneering study of psychology and group psychotherapy that has justly been regarded as a classic book in its field. "An interesting demonstration—and documentation—of this method in the words of the participants."—_The Kirkus Review._ Reprinted from the Rinehart edition.

_____ S-002-X **LOVE, HATE, FEAR, ANGER, AND OTHER**
$2.95 **LIVELY EMOTIONS,** by June Callwood.
Recently excerpted in the _Reader's Digest,_ this Doubleday reprint studies the human emotions, and shows how they master, or are mastered by, the individual.

_____ G-006-2 **THE IMPORTANCE OF FEELING INFERIOR,**
$2.95 by Marie Beynon Ray.
Ray shows how one's feelings of inferiority can be used to propel the individual to greater heights of achievement, and to guide each person to a richer, more productive life. Originally published by Harper & Row.

_____ G-009-7 **THE CONQUEST OF FEAR,** by Basil King.
$2.95 Inspired by the author's blindness, this reprint of the Doubleday edition provides a practical guide to overcoming the fears each person must face in their everyday life.

_____ W-013-5 **THE ORIGINS OF POPULAR SUPERSTITIONS**
$2.95 **AND CUSTOMS,** by T. Sharper Knowlson.
Knowlson's fascinating account of the follies of human belief includes sections on amulets, charms, divining rods, drinking customs, dreams and omens, crystal gazing, lucky stars, vampires, and much more. Complete with index.

_____ W-022-4 **MARRIAGE COUNSELING: FACT OR FALLACY?,**
$2.95 by Jerold R. Kuhn.
Dr. Kuhn provides a scholarly and timely treatment of a current topic, as drawn from actual case histories at the American Institute of Family Relations. The situations include minor communication problems, incompatibility, sexual dysfunction, and money worries. An original Newcastle publication.

_____ G-036-4 **YOUR HANDWRITING AND WHAT IT MEANS,**
$2.95 by William Leslie French.
An uncomplicated survey of the techniques of handwriting analysis, and how it can be used to reveal hidden character traits in oneself and others. Many signatures of noted personalities included.